Christopher Wordsworth

The Church of Ireland, Her History And Claims

Four Sermons Preached Before the University of Cambridge. Fourth

Edition

Christopher Wordsworth

The Church of Ireland, Her History And Claims
Four Sermons Preached Before the University of Cambridge. Fourth Edition

ISBN/EAN: 9783744753760

Printed in Europe, USA, Canada, Australia, Japan

Cover: Foto ©Lupo / pixelio.de

More available books at **www.hansebooks.com**

THE CHURCH OF IRELAND,

HER HISTORY AND CLAIMS:

ᚠour ᚠermons,

PREACHED

BEFORE THE UNIVERSITY OF CAMBRIDGE.

BY

CHR. WORDSWORTH, D.D. *Bishop of*

ARCHDEACON OF WESTMINSTER;

FORMERLY FELLOW OF TRINITY COLLEGE; PUBLIC ORATOR, AND
HULSEAN LECTURER IN THE UNIVERSITY.

FOURTH EDITION.

London,

RIVINGTONS, WATERLOO PLACE;

HIGH STREET, | TRINITY STREET,
Oxford. | Cambridge.

1868.

PREFACE.

SIXTEEN years ago the Author of this volume delivered a course of Sermons in Westminster Abbey on the History of the Church of Ireland, which were afterwards published in separate numbers, with copious notes, from trustworthy authorities, confirming and illustrating the statements made in the Sermons.

Some of the Sermons in that volume being out of print, the Author has been requested to republish them; but he has thought it better to recast them in a more compendious form, in which he might be dispensed from reproducing those historical authorities (which may be seen on reference to the former work), and in which he might also be enabled to avail himself of some valuable materials which have been brought to light since the appearance of his former publication.

In treating this subject, he has also endeavoured to deduce such practical reflections from the history of the Church of Ireland as seem to be suggested by it, and as appear to be not unseasonable at this juncture, and may render the study of that history more interesting and instructive to members of the United Church of England and Ireland at the present time.

Cloisters,
Westminster Abbey,
May 16, 1868.

CONTENTS.

SERMON I.

ON THE TIMES AND PREACHING OF ST. PATRICK.

PAGE

The subject proposed 1
The dignity and claims of a Christian Church, especially of
the Church of Ireland, upon England 2
The duty of studying her history—Introduction of Chris-
tianity into Ireland 2, 3
Mission of Palladius 3
St. PATRICK "the APOSTLE of Ireland;" materials for his
history 3
His "CONFESSION"—Meaning of the word 3, 4
Its design and character—Its Latinity 5
Facts deducible from it, as to the birth and parentage of St.
Patrick 5, 6
Carried captive at sixteen years of age as a slave to Ireland
—Description of his occupation and spiritual condition
at that time—Escapes from Ireland and returns home . 6
Resolves to go back to Ireland 7
His ordination—His character, teaching, and acts as a mis-
sionary Bishop, as described by a contemporary . . 7, 8
Dangers to which he was exposed in preaching to Ireland—
St. Patrick's "Epistle to Coroticus" 9
Its occasion—Its language, doctrinal and practical . 9, 10
Summary of his history 10, 11
Inferences from St. Patrick's history—Specially instructive
to the Christian Missionary 11, 12
Causes of his success in Ireland—His love for Christ—His
hymn—His love for the Scriptures 11
His spirit of prayer—His self-sacrifice—His prudence—His
knowledge of the Irish language 12
His deference to the Irish chiefs—His raising up of a native
Episcopate and Priesthood — Churches and Schools—
Fruits of his labours 13

PAGE

Appeal to St. Patrick for a settlement of the present religious differences in Ireland, as to Clerical celibacy—as to Church government 14

As to Christian Doctrine 14, 15

St. Patrick's Creed—Comparison of St. Patrick's Creed with the Creed of the present Church of Rome, commonly called the Trent Creed 15, 16

Not one of the Twelve Articles which are added in the Trent Creed to the Nicene Creed, was recognized by St. Patrick in his Creed or other writings — Inference from this fact 17

Prayer for Unity of all Classes in Ireland upon the basis of St. Patrick's Gospel, St. Patrick's Creed, and St. Patrick's Church 17, 18

Conclusion 18

SERMON II.

INTERVAL BETWEEN ST. PATRICK AND THE INVASION OF IRELAND BY KING HENRY II. OF ENGLAND.

Recapitulation 19

What St. Patrick had done, and what he had not been able to do 19, 20

His work was not rightly continued and completed by those who followed him—What ought to have been done—Christ's example—The Ancient Church of Ireland had Bishops but no Dioceses 20, 21

It developed itself in the collegiate and monastic form, not in the diocesan and parochial—Reason of this, and consequences—Ireland becomes the "University of the West" and the "Island of Saints"—Intellectual and spiritual benefits conferred by Ireland upon England 21, 22

Ireland the Seminary of Christian Missions to Scotland, England, and Continental Europe . . . . 21—23

St. Columba 21

Iona, or I-colm-kill 22

Its ancient glories 22, 23

St. Aidan and others 23

St. Columbanus 23

Darker side of the picture 23, 24

Parts of Ireland were then lapsing into barbarism—This due to the want of a Diocesan system—Erroneous theory of Congregationalism, as applied to Ireland—Practical application of this to the present state of the Church of

CONTENTS.   ix

CONTENTS.   ix

PAGE

England in her missionary work, both abroad and at
home 24, 25
Unhappy results of the feebleness of the Diocesan system of
England at the present time, exemplified in various par-
ticulars . . . . 25—28
Evils consequent on illegal and irregular introductions of
ritual innovations into the public service of God . 26—28
Benefits that would arise from a readjustment of the Diocesan
system of England 26, 27
Evils due to neglect of Diocesan Episcopacy in Ireland. 28, 29
Gradual process by which Romanism found its way into Ire-
land . . . . 29—31
The Danes—Their connexion with the Normans, and through
them with Rome—Gillebert the first Papal Legate in
Ireland—Introduction of Palls from Rome into Ireland. 30
Brief of Pope Hadrian IV. to Henry II. of England—Henry
invades Ireland, A.D. 1171 31
Brings it into subjection to Rome . . . 31, 32
Recapitulation 32
What ought then to have been done . . . 32, 33
What is " the old faith of Ireland "—What ought to be done
now 34
The glorious prospect now open to England and Ireland for
time and eternity. 34, 35

SERMON III.

INTERVAL BETWEEN THE ENGLISH INVASION OF IRELAND AND THE REFORMATION.

Ireland for four centuries, i. e. from the end of the twelfth
to the middle of the sixteenth century, had a Roman
Catholic Church Establishment — A Roman Catholic
Church Establishment proposed by some as a remedy for
the evils of Ireland—Appeal to numbers; is it conclu-
sive ? 37
Question proposed whether the Roman Catholic Church does
not disqualify itself from being a religious establishment 38
Its influence on Christianity, and consequently on the peace
and safety of Nations 38, 39
Its system with regard to the Confessional and to Oaths—
The Oaths of Roman Catholic Bishops to persecute
Protestants 39
The relation of Rome to Protestant Princes . . 39, 40
Union with the Church of Rome,—is it possible for the
Church of England ? 40

a

PAGE

Not a question of detail, but of principles . . 40, 41
The opposite foundations of the two Churches . . 41, 42
But why should not a conference take place between members
    of the two Churches in Ireland?—Basis of union . . 44
The question of Romish Establishment in Ireland not to be
    argued merely on *à priori* grounds—The experiment
    has been tried for a long time 43
What were its results?—Spiritual condition of Ireland *before*
    the Roman Catholic Establishment in Ireland contrasted
    with its condition *under* it—Appeal made for proof to
    two public authentic state documents, emanating from
    Roman Catholics—The first document, the Petition of
    Irish Roman Catholic Nobles in Ireland to the Pope,
    A.D. 1318 44
Their account of their own miserable condition under Anglo-
    Romish rule 44, 45
Did the Pope apply any remedy? 45
The second document, the celebrated "Statute of Kilkenny,"
    A.D. 1367—Enactments in that statute, of English
    Roman Catholic Bishops and others in Ireland, against
    the Irish Roman Catholics—Did the Pope mediate be-
    tween them?—What his nominees did do . . . 46
To what the calamities of Ireland are *not* due—*Not* due to
    any repugnance on her part to the Holy Scriptures, and
    to the pure Catholic faith and primitive form of Church
    Government . . . . . ! . . 47, 48
Not due to any love for Papal Supremacy in itself—*Not* due
    to any hatred of the Reformation, as such . . . 48
To *what* the calamities of Ireland are due? This question
    answered 48, 49
The Reformation has not failed in Ireland; the Reformation
    has not been rejected by Ireland 49
Who have failed in Ireland?—And in what respect?—How
    England has failed in denying vernacular Scriptures and
    a vernacular Liturgy to Ireland: proof of this . 49, 50
Unhappy consequences of her failure in this and other respects 50
The Papacy took advantage of the failure; its cruel measures
    against England—Incitements to rebellion . . 50, 51
Origin of the Romish Episcopate in Ireland—Sanguinary ex-
    ultation of the spirit of rebellion 51
How the Reformation was presented to Ireland, and how it
    ought to have been presented to Ireland but was not 51, 52
Practical reflections suggested by this historical review 53, 54

SERMON IV.

ON THE CHURCH OF IRELAND AS A NATIONAL RELIGIOUS ESTABLISHMENT.

PAGE

Question proposed—What it is *not* 55
What it *is* 56
Scriptural grounds for National Establishments of true religion 57
Objections to the Church of Ireland as the religious Esta-
blishment of that country—"It is a new Institution;"
"The Reformation has failed" . . . . "has been
rejected" in Ireland; Answer 58
Who has failed in Ireland?—How England has dealt with
the Reformation and the Church in Ireland—As to
vernacular Scriptures and a vernacular Liturgy—With
regard to Tithe property 59
With regard to Church preferments in Ireland — With
regard to residences for the Clergy 60
What the cause for wonder is 60, 61
And yet what is done and said by many in England? . . 61
What our duty to Ireland is 62
Objection against the Church of Ireland, derived from
Tables of Population; Answer 62, 63
Is the appeal to the Census relevant to the question at
issue? 63
Appeal to Holy Scripture and ancient Church history . 63, 64
Argument from numbers—What are Tables of Population? 64
Application to Ireland 64, 65
Fallacy in the reference to them 65
What is a sure sign of moral degeneracy? . . . 65, 66
What is a sure sign of magnanimity?—Objection to the
Church of Ireland from the fewness of her members in
some parishes 66
Answers to this objection 66, 67
There is no Christian in Ireland who is not interested in the
maintenance of the Church, and who does not derive
some benefit from her 67, 68
Objection to the Church of Ireland, that it is unjust that she
should be maintained by payments from Roman Ca-
tholics, who derive no benefit from her . . . 68
Answer 69, 70
What is the first duty of a Church?—How is its useful-

PAGE

ness to be tested?—Application to the Church of Rome
in Ireland 71
Application to the Church of Ireland—Contrast—Inference
therefrom 72
To whom do the Tithes in Ireland belong? 73
Is England prepared to rob Almighty God, and to take up
arms against Him? 73, 74
Character of the present times 74
Practical inferences therefrom—Prospects before us . . 75
Warning and exhortation 75, 76
Conclusion 77

SERMON I.

JOB viii. 8. 10.

"Inquire, I pray thee, of the former age, and prepare thyself
to the search of their fathers: shall not they teach thee, and tell
thee, and utter words out of their heart?"

IT is my purpose, in the discourses which, with God's
help, I may be permitted to deliver in this place on
the Sundays of the present month, to invite your
attention to the history of the CHURCH of IRELAND,
and to her claims on our sympathy and help at this
time.

Jesus Christ[1] is "King of kings, and Lord of
lords." To Him "all power on earth is given."
"All kings shall bow down before Him, and all nations
shall do Him service." And a Church of Christ is a
holy thing. If she is faithful to Christ, He loves her
as His own Body and Spouse[2], and whosoever persecutes her, persecutes Him[3], Who will judge the world.
But whoever is willing to spend and be spent for her
in her hour of danger and distress, will receive a blessing from Christ, who has knit His members together
in one communion and fellowship, and who says by
His holy Apostle, "If one member suffer, the other
members suffer with it[4]."

[1] Rev. xvii. 14; xix. 16. Matt. xxviii. 18. Ps. lxxii. 11. Phil.
ii. 10.
[2] Acts xx. 28. Eph. v. 28, 29.
[3] Acts ix. 4.   [4] 1 Cor. xii. 26.

B

Brethren, if such is our duty to every Christian Church, we are bound by special obligations to perform it to the Church of Ireland.

The misfortunes of the Church of Ireland (I speak it advisedly) are due in a great measure to England; and we ought not to aggravate her sufferings by harsh language and ruthless spoliation; rather, we owe her a large measure of reparation and redress. We are also united to her by holy ties of Christian faith, and by solemn pledges of public honour; and her maintenance as a national institution is identified with our own, and with the nearest and dearest interests of our common country and common Christianity.

In order to appreciate the claims of Christ's Church in Ireland, we must know her history. We owe her this debt of justice. That history will display to us noble examples of self-sacrifice for Christ. It is fraught with instruction to Churches and nations. May the Great Head of the Church enable us so to read it, that it may conduce to His glory and to the advancement of His truth, and to the salvation of our souls and those of others. May the Holy Spirit of Peace enlighten us, and keep far from us all prejudice and bitterness, so that, in all that we say on this sacred subject, we may speak the truth in love [5].

The time when the Gospel was first preached in Ireland is hid in obscurity. Some ancient writers [6] affirm that it was introduced there in the Apostolic age. This however is certain, that in the year of our Lord 431, a Christian Bishop named Palladius was sent thither by Celestine, Bishop of Rome [7], probably

---

[5] Eph. iv. 15.

[6] Euseb. Dem. Evang. iii. 9. St. Chrysostom, tom. vi. p. 635; viii. p. 111, ed. Savil. St. Columbanus, Epist. ad Bonifac. § 10. Lanigan, Eccl. Hist. i. p. 2.

[7] See St. Prosper Aquitanus in Chronico ad A.D. 431, and Contra Collatorem in the Appendix to St. Augustine's works, tom. x. pt. ii. Append. p. 196. The passages may be seen in Dr. Todd's

with the help of St. German, Bishop of Auxerre in Gaul, who had twice visited Britain, in order to repress the Pelagian heresy.

The mission of Palladius was of brief duration, and produced little fruit[8]. But only a short time elapsed before another person visited Ireland, who is universally recognized as the Apostle of that country. That person was ST. PATRICK.

The history of St. Patrick has been disfigured by many fabulous legends[9], of comparatively recent date; but happily we possess authentic records of his life and teaching, from his own hand.

The principal of these is called his CONFESSION[10].

The meaning of this title must not be misunderstood. The word *Confession*, as used by St. Patrick, means a public acknowledgment of God's grace; a thankful recognition of His mercies, and an ascription of praise for them. It means also a profession of the faith which the writer held, and of the doctrine which he taught in Ireland.

This use of the word *confession* may be illustrated by St. Paul's language in his Epistle to the Romans, " As I live, saith the Lord, every knee shall bow to Me, and every tongue shall *confess* to God[1]." " For this cause

valuable work, " St. Patrick, Apostle of Ireland," Dublin, 1864, pp. 269—273; cp. ibid. p. 275. See also Bede, Hist. Eccl. i. 13, with Professor Hussey's notes.

[8] St. Patrick, in his Confession, § 18, says that till his time " the Irish had no knowledge of God, and only worshipped unclean idols."

[9] As the learned Roman Catholic Historian Tillemont affirms, Mémoires, pour servir à l'Histoire Ecclés. xvi. p. 782, in his Life of St. Patrick, where he says that there is " rien de certain" in the popular lives of St. Patrick; cp. the Rev. Robert King's excellent Irish Church History, p. 13.

[10] Published first by Sir James Ware, Lond. 1656, reprinted in Gallandii Bibl. Patr. vol. x. p. 159, by Dr. Villanueva, in Sancti Patricii Opuscula, Dublin, 1835, and in Abbé Migne's Patrologia, vol. liii. p. 802. For testimonies to its genuineness, see Dr. Todd's St. Patrick, p. 347.

[1] Rom. xiv. 11.

I will *confess* to Thee among the Gentiles, and will
sing unto Thy Name²." And again, "With the heart
man believeth unto righteousness, and with the mouth
confession is made unto salvation³."

This work was written by St. Patrick in his old age,
and he bequeathed it as a legacy to the Church. His
design in writing it was, that posterity might know
what he had done and taught⁴; and that all might also
know, that, although he had been permitted to labour
in Ireland for many years, and had baptized many
thousands there⁵, and had planted many Churches in
that country, yet he claimed no honour for himself, but
ascribed all the glory to God.

"What shall I render to God," he says⁶, "for all
His benefits? I have no strength but from Him. I
am ready to receive at His hands the cup of sorrow
which He delivers to those who love Him. God grant
that I may never lose the flock which He has given
me. May He vouchsafe me perseverance to the end,
and grace to shed my blood for His name's sake!
This I know will be true gain—it will be Life Eternal."

"I protest" (he says at the close of that work), "in
truth and in joy, in the presence of God and His holy
angels, that it was for the sake of the Gospel and its
promises, and for no other reason, that I came back to
that country (Ireland) from which I had formerly
escaped. I beseech all who believe in God, and who

² Rom. xv. 9.
³ Rom. x. 10. That this is the meaning of the word 'confessio,' corresponding to the Greek ὁμολογία, is clear from
numerous sentences in the work itself, e.g. c. 2, where he says,
"I cannot keep in silence so great benefits and such grace as the
Lord has vouchsafed to me in the land of my captivity (Ireland),
because this is my reward, to be exalted after tribulation and
acknowledgment of God, and to *confess* His marvellous works
before every nation under Heaven." The Latin verb 'confiteor'
is used four times in this chapter; and the cognate sense of profession of faith in the second chapter of the "Confession."
⁴ Confession, § 6.
⁵ Confession, § 2. "In Domino baptizavi tot millia hominum."
⁶ Confession, § 23.

pray to Him and fear Him, and who vouchsafe to read this book, which I, Patrick, a sinner and unlearned, have written in Ireland; let no one ever say that any little that I have done or taught there, according to God's good pleasure, was due to me and my ignorance. But judge ye rather this, and be ye fully persuaded, that it was God who wrought by me. . . . This is my confession before I die."

In order that this confession of God's power and love might be more generally known, St. Patrick wrote it in Latin. For a long time he hesitated before he could make up his mind to write in that language. He had been many years in Ireland, and had little opportunity of cultivating the Latin tongue. "I feel shame and fear," he says, "to display my own rudeness of speech; and because I cannot express clearly in that language what my heart feels, and what my spirit burns to declare[7]."

But his love and thankfulness to God overcame his bashfulness; and the rude simplicity of the Latin style in which the Confession is written gives additional value and interest to it. It confirms the proof of its genuineness; and reminds the reader that the author was not tutored in schools of human learning; while the facts recorded in it show that he was "a good man, full of the Holy Ghost," and that he was a blessed instrument in God's hands for the promotion of His truth.

St. Patrick was born in Britain[8], probably in a village of Scotland, upon the banks of the Clyde, between Dumbarton and Glasgow. He tells us that his father was a Deacon of the Church, and his grandfather a Priest[9]. His father held office also as a

[7] See Confession, § 4 and § 5.

[8] Not Brittany in France. I have examined that opinion in another place, Occasional Sermons, pp. 31, 32, and notes. Ireland was commonly called Scotland (Scotia) till the twelfth century, and the Irish were called Scots (Scoti) till that time.

[9] Conf. § 1.

magistrate[1], and was of a good family[2]. When St.
Patrick was sixteen years of age, his native country
was a prey to the Slave Trade. It was invaded by a
barbarous horde of bandits; and he, with many thousands more[3], was carried captive and sold as a slave
into Ireland. He served a heathen master there in a
wild country, given up to idolatry[4], and he was sent
to the woods and hills to feed cattle. In his Confession, he draws an affecting picture of his condition at
that time. " Often," he says[5], "in wintry nights I
wandered as a shepherd on the mountains of Ireland."
But in his loneliness he felt God's presence, and had
sweet communings with Him. In the land of his
captivity and friendlessness, under the genial influence
of sky and stars, the blessed truths of the Gospel,
which had been planted by his parents in his mind, but
had lain dormant there, awoke within him. " Often,"
he says, " I abode on the hills and in the forests, and
arose before dawn to pray. I was drenched by rain,
and chilled by snow and frost; but my spirit glowed
within me, and I prayed more frequently. . . ." Thus
by means of slavery he became the freeman of Christ;
and banishment from his country brought him home to
God. Six years passed away; he then escaped from
captivity in Ireland, and returned to his native land.
His parents and friends in Britain received him joy-
fully; and entreated him with tears, that after so
many afflictions, he would never leave them more[6].

But God had ordered it otherwise. St. Patrick had
seen the people of Ireland scattered like sheep without
a shepherd. He had seen them bowing down before
idols[7]; and his heart was moved within him. He
seems to have had a special call from God to preach
the Gospel there[8]. With a noble spirit of Christian

---

[1] Decurio; Epist. ad Corot. § 5.
[2] Ibid. "Vendidi nobilitatem meam pro utilitate aliorum."
[3] Conf. § 1.   [4] Conf. § 16, § 18.
[5] Conf. § 6.   [6] Conf. § 10, § 15.
[7] Conf. § 16, § 18.   [8] Conf. § 10. ·

forgiveness he resolved to render good for evil, and to leave the joys and honours of home, and to encounter hardship, scorn, persecution[9], and, it might be, death itself, in order to deliver Ireland from idolatry, and to win that country to Christ, where he had been an exile and a slave. God blessed his resolve. He was admitted to the holy orders of Deacon, Priest, and Bishop. He does not mention by whom[1]. Certain it is that he was not sent by Rome[2]. His mission in Ireland seems to have begun about A.D. 440[3], and there he spent the remainder of his life, about 50 years. In that time he traversed the greater part of Ireland, preaching the Gospel, baptizing the natives, planting Churches, ordaining Bishops, Priests, and Deacons. "I owe," he says in his Confession[4], "a great debt of thanks to God, who granted me this grace, that by my means multitudes are born again in the Lord, and are afterwards admitted to the holy Eucharist, and that Clergy are ordained every where for those who embrace the faith."

One of the Bishops who were consecrated by him, and who appears to have been his own nephew, and whose name was Sechnall, or (in a Latin form) Secundinus, Bishop of Armagh[5], composed a short Latin poem, still extant[6], which describes the acts of St. Patrick. In

---

[9] See Conf. § 15, § 16, and Epist. ad Corot. § 1.

[1] Probably it was by St. German, of Auxerre. In a very ancient Hymn it is stated that St. Patrick studied the canons under St. German. See Occasional Sermons, p. 34 and notes; and the authorities in Mr. King's Irish Church History, pp. 28—30; and Dr. Todd's St. Patrick, pp. 313, 314. St. German having twice visited Britain, may have been known at least by name to St. Patrick's father; and St. Patrick, in his Confession, expresses a wish to visit his brethren in France, whom he calls 'sanctos Domini mei,' § 19.

[2] See Occasional Sermons, pp. 35—38, and Dr. Todd's St. Patrick, pp. 309—313.

[3] For the evidence in favour of this date, rather than A.D. 432, see Dr. Todd's St. Patrick, pp. 391—396.

[4] Conf. § 16, and § 32.

[5] Dr. Todd's St. Patrick, p. 364.

[6] It is a "Hymnus Alphabeticus" in rude tetrameter trochaic.

it the Author says that St. Patrick was stedfast in the
fear of God, and immoveable in the faith of God, upon
whom the Church is built, as upon a rock [7], and that
he received his Apostleship from God [8]. "God sent
him forth as His Apostle," he adds, "as He sent St.
Paul to the Gentiles. Humble he was, through fear
of God, both in spirit and in body, and he gloried only
in the Cross of Christ. Boldly he proclaimed the
name of God to the heathen, and gave them the everlasting grace of the laver of salvation; and, after the
pattern of Christ, he was ready to lay down his life for
the flock. Therefore the Saviour exalted him to be chief
among His Priests, in order that he might admonish the
Clergy in their heavenly warfare. He found the divine
treasure in the Sacred Volume—the Holy Scriptures—
and he beheld the Saviour's Godhead in His flesh. A
faithful witness of God he was in the Catholic faith,
the words of which are stored up in the Divine oracles [9].
A true and noble husbandman he was of the Evangelical field, the seed of which is the Gospel of Christ;
he sowed that seed with divine speech into the ears of
the wise, and ploughed their hearts by the help of the
Holy Ghost. Therefore Christ chose him as His vicar
upon earth, to deliver captives from a double bondage;
from the slavery of men, and the dominion of the

It was first printed by Colgan in 1647, afterwards by Sir James
Ware, 1656, also by Villanueva, "Opuscula S. Patricii," Dublin,
1835; and with a learned Introduction and notes by Dr. Todd in
his "Book of Hymns of the Ancient Irish Church," Dublin, 1855,
p. 11. It is a valuable companion to St. Patrick's Confessio, and
Epistola ad Coroticum. It seems to have been written while
St. Patrick was still living, for the verbs which refer to him are
in the *present* tense. See Dr. Todd's edition, pp. 40, 41.

[7] The original is "ut petrum;" and the reference is to the
places in Scripture where Christ is called the Foundation-stone,
or Corner-stone of the Church (Isa. xxviii. 16. Eph. ii. 20.
1 Pet. ii. 6); and the Rock of the Church (Matt. xvi. 18).

[8] Hymnus S. Secundini, *v.* 9. 11.

[9] A testimony from ancient Ireland to the supremacy and
sufficiency of Holy Scripture.

devil. He held the faith in the Trinity of the Sacred
Name, and taught that there is One substance in
Three Persons; and by day and by night, having his
loins girt with the girdle of the Lord, he prayed to the
Lord his God, from whom he will hereafter receive
the reward of his labours, with the Apostles of Christ."

Such is the testimony to St. Patrick from one of his
own contemporaries.

That these labours were performed amid many
dangers not only from the heathen tribes of Ireland
but also from foreign aggression, appears from another
work, still extant, of St. Patrick himself.

This is an Epistle [1] of remonstrance which he wrote
to the emissaries of a certain chieftain called Coroticus,
probably of Wales [2] or of Cornwall, who had invaded
Ireland, and pillaged it, and carried captive many of
the Christians of the churches planted by St. Patrick.
" I do not wish," he says, "to open my mouth with
words of sternness, but I am constrained by zeal for
God and the truth, and by love for my friends and
children in the faith, for whom I have given up my
country and my kindred, and am ready to give up my
life, if God thinks me worthy. I have made a vow to
my God that I will preach the Gospel to the heathen.
O Lord! what shall I do? Thy sheep are torn in
pieces before my eyes by robbers, at the command of
Coroticus, not fearing God nor the priests whom God
has chosen, and to whom He has given power that
what they bind on earth should be bound in heaven [3].
Savage wolves are devouring the flock of Christ, *that*
flock in Ireland which was lately so prosperous. They
have filled their houses with the spoils of Christians.
But thus they reap death to themselves; all who work

---

[1] The "Epistola S. Patricii ad Coroticum," or rather "ad
Corotici subditos," was printed by Sir James Ware in 1656, and
by Villanueva in 1835 in Opuscula S. Patricii, p. 240.

[2] Cp. Todd's St. Patrick, p. 352.

[3] Epist. ad Corot. § 3. Matt. xvi. 19; xviii. 18

wickedness procure for themselves eternal death, and
everlasting punishment [4]. The Church," he adds,
"mourns for her children, she weeps for those who
have not yet been slain by the sword, but have been
carried away captive. I weep for you, my most fair
and loving brethren, a countless multitude whom I
have begotten in Christ. I weep also for the dead.
I weep for you, my beloved; but yet I rejoice also;
my labours among you, and journeys have not been in
vain, God be thanked; ye have believed and been baptized, and ye have passed from this world into Paradise [5]. I see with mine eyes that ye have migrated to
that place where is neither darkness, nor mourning,
nor death; and ye will reign hereafter in glory with
Apostles, and Prophets, and Martyrs. But where will
then they be, who rebel against Christ? Where will
Coroticus be, with his savage crew? Sinners and
spoilers will perish from the presence of the Lord, but
the just will rejoice with Christ, and judge the nations,
and have dominion for evermore. I protest before
God and His holy Angels, that so it will be. 'He
who believeth shall be saved, but he that believeth not,
will be damned.' God hath spoken it [6]. I entreat
that this letter of mine may be read in the presence of
all the people and of Coroticus himself. May God
touch their hearts, that they may repent! They have
acted as murderers against the brethren of the Lord;
but let them repent, and set at liberty the Christians
whom they have taken prisoners; so they themselves
may live to God and be saved for evermore. Amen [7]."

Such was St. Patrick's courage. He feared God;
he feared not men; he feared not death; he was ready,
he was eager, to meet it, for the sake of Christ, and the
Gospel, and of those souls, for whom Christ died, and

[4] Epist. ad Corot. § 7.
[5] Not Purgatory. Epist. ad Corot. § 9.
[6] Mark xvi. 16. St. Patrick speaks here of Christ as God.
[7] Epist. ad Corot. § 10, § 11.

who were his own spiritual offspring. At length God
took him to Himself. God had blessed his labours
with an abundant harvest; he never quitted the field,
and full of years and of good works, and like a reaper
with his sheaves around him, he fell asleep in Christ.

Brethren, let us apply these things to ourselves.
The history of St. Patrick is instructive to all.
Since the days of the holy Apostles, few missionary
works have been so signally blessed as his labours in
Ireland.

What were the causes of his success?

First and foremost must be placed his love for
Christ. This feeling is beautifully expressed in St.
Patrick's Irish Hymn, probably " the oldest monu-
ment of the Irish language now in existence[8]."

" May Christ be with me, Christ before me,
  Christ behind me, Christ within me,
  Christ beneath me, Christ above me;
  Christ at my right hand, Christ at my left hand.
        *   *   *   *   *

" May Christ be in the heart of every man who thinks of me;
  Christ in the mouth of every man who speaks to me;
  Christ in every eye that sees me;
  Christ in every ear that hears me."

Next, his love for the Holy Scriptures.

His two extant works abound with references to the
Word of God[9], and they are animated throughout with
its spirit. The Word of God was his Book of books,
it was his rule of faith and life, it was his daily bread.

Next must be mentioned his fervency in prayer.
Even when a boy of sixteen, feeding cattle on the hills

[8] King's History, p. 40. See Todd's St. Patrick, pp. 426—429.
[9] The passages of Scripture are quoted from a Latin version,
older than St. Jerome. A proof of the antiquity and genuineness
of the Confession. The same remark applies to the Epistle to
Coroticus.
   Another evidence of the antiquity and genuineness of these
works may be seen in the fact that the author claims no miracu-
lous powers for St. Patrick. How different are they in this
respect from the mediæval lives of St. Patrick! Cp. Dr. Todd,
p. 387.

of Ireland, he, like David feeding sheep in the fields of
Bethlehem, had continual communings with God. His
heart was in heaven. Thence he derived faith and
love, joy and peace, patience, strength, and courage.

No wonder that after his return to his home in
Scotland he still yearned for Ireland; he had seen her
wretchedness, the wretchedness of heathen idolatry.
He felt compassion for her, and longed to win her to
Christ. Christ was his all in all. Burning with love
of Christ, and of the souls for whom He died, and full
of His Spirit, and following His example, he forgave
and forgot the hard usage he had endured there; he
renounced the joys of home and came back to Ireland.
He laboured there among many hardships and dangers,
his life being often in jeopardy [10], during fifty years,
spending and being spent for Christ.

This was the Lord's doing. "Not I, but God in
me and by me," was his language; "to God be all the
praise." Humble he was, but courageous; meek and
gentle, but resolute and intrepid. Nothing he was in
his own eyes, but strong in faith in God. Therefore
God gave him more grace. After a long life he died
in peace, a Martyr in will, a constant Confessor of the
Faith.

While we remember his zeal, we must not forget
the wisdom by which it was guided. Here also he is
an example to all Christian missionaries.

He had learnt the language of Ireland in his youth,
in his six years' sojourn there. This was one cause of
his success. Ireland was then occupied by different
clans. Wisely he addressed himself first to the chieftains of the clans. He converted many of them to

---

[10] See Dr. Todd's St. Patrick, p. 502; and especially the words
of St. Patrick's "Irish Hymn," where he prays to Christ for
daily protection (p. 428):—

> "Christ protect me to-day,
> Against poison, against burning,
> Against drowning, against wounds,
> Against every hostile savage power,
> Directed against my body and my soul."

the faith, and baptized them and their sons and daughters. This was the seminary of the ancient Irish Church. From among the chieftains and their families he raised up a native Priesthood and a native Episcopate in Ireland [1]. He planted a native Church with a native ministry. He built houses of God, in which prayers and intercessions went up continually to heaven for those among whom he dwelt, who were won to Christ and the Gospel by holy offices of love, and the daily ministries of religion. Those daily ministries in the churches, schools, and colleges founded by him, prepared the inmates of those Christian households to become teachers of the truth [2]. Thus Ireland was supplied with priests and bishops from among her own people; and the results of this wise system were seen in the stream of Christian missions, the glory of Ireland, which flowed from her in the sixth and seventh centuries to evangelize Britain and other countries of Europe [3].

In another important respect, St. Patrick's history is full of instruction. It seems to offer a solution of the religious difficulties, and a settlement of the religious differences which now unhappily prevail in Ireland.

St. Patrick is acknowledged on all sides to be "the Apostle of Ireland."

Let us therefore appeal to him.

[1] Cp. Dr. Todd's St. Patrick, p. 28.
[2] The dangers, to which St. Patrick and his followers were exposed, obliged him to concentrate his converts for common support in conventual buildings, from which women were not excluded ("mulierum administrationem et societatem non abnuebant," is the testimony of the ancient author of the "Catalogus Sanctorum Hiberniæ;" see Dr. Todd's work, p. 88, note), and these buildings were often strongly fortified. See Dr. Todd's St. Patrick, pp. 502—504, and pp. 28—38, and p. 88 note, and p. 93. Hence the Round Towers in Ireland: Dr. Reeves, Act. of Abp. Colton, p. 88.
[3] See the next Discourse; and the sketch of St. Patrick's Missionary work, in Dr. Todd's volume, pp. 502—506.

He tells us that his father was a Deacon of the Church, and his grandfather a Priest. Here is a proof that the celibacy, which Rome now enforces on all her clergy, was no part of Church discipline in the days of Ireland's Apostle. With regard to Church government, St. Patrick informs us that he himself was a Bishop; and he ordained Priests and Deacons; he mentions these three orders of Ministers of the Church —and no other. Scotland, Ireland, and England were united in the same form of Church government in the age of St. Patrick, and for a thousand years after it. Why should they not join together in the same bond of union now?

And what was his Doctrine?

Holy Scripture was his rule of faith [4]. But he well knew that the *true sense* of Scripture *is Scripture;* and his converts were not to be left to gather that sense from the Bible without the help of the Church. He therefore sets down his profession of faith with his own hand [5]. It bears a strong resemblance to the Nicene Creed. "There is no other God," he says, "nor ever was, nor ever will be, besides the Father, Who is unbegotten and without beginning, and from Whom every beginning is, and His Son Jesus Christ, Whom we acknowledge to have been always with the Father, before the beginning of the world; begotten ineffably [6] before every beginning; and by Him were made things visible and invisible, and He was made man, and overcame death, and was received up into heaven to the Father, Who hath given Him all power above every Name of things in heaven, and things in earth, and things under the earth, that every tongue should confess that Jesus Christ is Lord, to the glory of God the Father [7]. We believe in Him, and look for his speedy Coming to judge the quick and dead, when He will render to every man according to his works. He has shed upon us abundantly the gift of the Holy Spirit, the pledge

[4] See above, p. 8.
[5] Confession, § 2.
[6] Inenarrabiliter.
[7] Phil. ii. 10. Col. i. 16, 17.

of Immortality, Who makes men to believe and to obey, that they may be sons of God the Father, Whom we confess; and we worship One God in the Trinity of the Sacred Name [8]. And we firmly believe," he says [9], " that we shall rise again in the glory of Jesus Christ; being fellow-heirs with Him, and conformed to His likeness; for 'of Him, and through Him, and in Him are all things [1].' To Him be glory for evermore! ' "

Such is the Creed of St. Patrick, set down with his own hand, nearly fourteen hundred years ago, at the close of his long life, in the writing which he left as a last bequest to Ireland and the world.

What therefore shall we now say?

May we be permitted, with all affectionate respect, to address our Roman Catholic brethren in Ireland?

Take the Creed of St. Patrick in one hand, and take the present Creed of the Church of Rome, commonly called the Trent Creed [2], in the other. Place them side by side. The Trent Creed is now imposed by the

[8] Compare the last words of the Epistle to Coroticus, ed. Villanueva, p. 247, and St. Patrick's "Irish Hymn" (called his Lorica or breastplate, as describing his Christian armour), in Dr. Todd's volume, p. 426:—

> " I bind on myself (as a breastplate) to-day
> The strong power of an invocation of the Trinity,
> The faith of the Trinity in Unity."
> " I bind on myself to-day
> The power of the Incarnation of Christ,
>   With that of His Baptism;
> The power of the Crucifixion,
>   With that of His Burial;
> The power of the Resurrection,
>   With the Ascension;
> The power of the Coming to the sentence of Judgment."

This noble Hymn—the "Te Deum" of Ireland—may be combined with his "Confessio," as showing what St. Patrick's faith and teaching were.

[9] Conf. § 23.   [1] Rom. xi. 36. Col. i. 16, 17.

[2] Or Creed of Pope Pius IV. A.D. 1564, called "Forma Juramenti;" see Bullarium Romanum, tom. iv. part ii. pp. 201. 204, ed. Rom. 1715.

Church of Rome, in the form of an oath, on her ecclesiastics. She asserts that it is "the Catholic Faith,
out of which is no salvation." And she requires all
converts to Romanism to say, "I declare that all who
contravene this creed are deserving of everlasting malediction [3]." In that Trent Creed, she has added twelve
articles to the Nicene Creed, which we hold. .Look
now at the Creed of St. Patrick,—Do you find those
twelve articles there? One of those articles is the
assertion of Roman supremacy, and that the Church
of Rome is "the Mother and Mistress of all Churches."
That is the foundation of the Roman system. Do you
find that there? No. The words Roman See, Roman
Bishop, Roman Church, do not once occur in the Creed
of St. Patrick, nor in any of his writings [4]. Another
of the twelve Trent Articles is Transubstantiation.
Do you find that in St. Patrick's Creed? No. Another
is Purgatory. Do you find that there? No [5]. Another
is Invocation of Saints [6]. Do you find that there?

---

[3] See the Roman Pontifical, p. 455, ed. Rom. 1818.

[4] As to the Canon ascribed to St. Patrick, "Si quæ quæstiones
in hâc insulâ oriantur, ad sedem Apostolicam referantur," let me
refer to what is said in another place : Occasional Sermons, pp. 53,
54. That this Canon is not due to St. Patrick has been shown by
Mr. King : Primacy of Armagh, p. 14. Dr. Todd asserts (p. 485)
that "it is scarcely possible to receive these Canons as really his."
See his remarks, pp. 485—489. There is a remarkable Latin
document, probably not later than the eighth century, which is
entitled, "A Catalogue of Saints of Ireland, according to their
divers times." It says, "The first order was in the times of St.
Patrick; they had one Head (caput), Christ; one leader (ducem),
Patrick." Nothing is said of Rome. See Ussher's Works, vi.
477. King's History, p. 60. Todd's St. Patrick, p. 88.

[5] He says that the souls of the faithful go at death to Paradise.
Epist. ad Corot. § 9.

[6] In the passage of the Confession where we read "unde venit
ignoro, ut spiritu *Eliam* invocarem" (§ 9), Elias may perhaps be
the Hebrew name for *God*, El; see Matt. xxvii. 47, Dr. Todd's
St. Patrick, pp. 371—373, and notes; and King's Church History of Ireland, i. 46. To the passages quoted by them may be
added the line from the Basle altar-p.ece, now in the Hôtel Cluny
at Paris :—

No. Another is Communion in one kind. Do you find that there? No. Another is the doctrine of Indulgences. Do you find that there? No. In a word, do you find a single one of those twelve articles there? No; not one. And yet it is asserted by the Church of Rome that a belief in every one of these twelve articles is necessary to salvation; and she denounces us as heretics and schismatics, because we do not and cannot receive them. What! if all these twelve articles are necessary to salvation, how is it that St. Patrick, in setting down his own Confession of Faith, and in recounting the doctrine which he preached to the people of Ireland, does not mention one of them? How is it that he does not specify a single one of those twelve articles in any part of his writings? Was St. Patrick a heretic? If so, we are content to be heretics with him. Was St. Patrick a schismatic? We are content to be schismatics with him. We are satisfied with his Creed. We hold every article of it. And we earnestly entreat you to consider, whether, if you are not content with St. Patrick's Creed, you ought to claim St. Patrick as your Apostle? Or, if you claim St. Patrick as your Apostle, you ought not to be content with your Apostle's Creed?

Finally, may it please God of His great mercy to raise up many among us, animated with the spirit of St. Patrick! May it please Him to raise up many full of love for Christ and for the Holy Scriptures, men of prayer, zealous for Christ and for His flock; men meek and humble, and yet bold and resolute, com-

"Quis sicut (sic) *El* fortis, Soter, medicus benedictus?"
But it is strange that any stress should be laid upon that passage of the Confession, for St. Patrick himself says there that he did not know how it came to pass that he made such an invocation at all; and whatever it was, it was uttered in his sleep.
The absence from St. Patrick's Creed, and from St. Patrick's writings, of any reference whatever to the Blessed Virgin Mary, who is now made a principal—if not *the* principal—object of devotion by the Church of Rome, is very worthy of notice.

passionate and tender-hearted, ready to forgive injuries
and to render good for evil, and yet firm and unflinch-
ing in the maintenance of the truth, and glad to lay
down their lives for it, in the blessed hope of a joyful
immortality. Let national antipathies be laid aside ;
let the names of sects and parties be forgotten ; "let
not Ephraim vex Judah, nor Judah vex Ephraim."
Let England and Ireland be true to themselves, to one
another, and to God ; let them be united on the common ground of St. Patrick's Gospel, St. Patrick's
Creed, and St. Patrick's Church.   Let them dwell
together in unity, in the serene and peaceful atmosphere
of Evangelical Truth, Apostolical order, and Catholic
love !

SERMON II.

MARK vi. 39.

" JESUS commanded them to make all sit down by companies upon the green grass."

IN the foregoing discourse on the history of Christianity in Ireland, evidence was given of the blessed work which Almighty God wrought in that country, in the fifth century after Christ, by the hands of St. Patrick, who has been justly called " the Apostle of Ireland."

Strong in faith, mighty in the Scriptures, full of love for Christ and the souls for which He died, and not relying on himself, but on God's grace, and ascribing all the glory of his actions to Him; not holding his life dear to himself, but ready to lay it down for Christ and His flock, in the hope of a joyful immortality, St. Patrick laboured for about half a century in preaching the Gospel to Ireland.

Such fair beginnings promised much fruit. How was it, that this fruit was not brought to perfection, and that much of it was blighted and withered?

This is a question which will be found instructive to ourselves; and will now engage our attention, while we proceed to survey the interval of time between the death of St. Patrick, near the end of the fifth century, and the invasion of Ireland by King Henry II. of

c 2

England, in the latter part of the twelfth century after Christ [1].

St. Patrick had broken up the fallow ground of Ireland with the plough of missionary tillage ; but he had not time to enclose the fields. He had brought many wandering sheep home to Christ ; but he had not been able to mark out the sheepwalks, and to finish the work of building folds for the flock.

What ought then to have been done ?

Our blessed Lord has taught us. He was about to feed the multitudes on the mountain. Though they were hungry, they must wait till they had been grouped and arranged in order. He would not feed them as a mixed crowd. They must first be planted, to use St. Mark's metaphor, like a garden well laid out in *parterres* [2]. "He commanded His disciples to make them all sit down in companies upon the green grass." He then blessed the loaves, and fed the people by the ministry of His Apostles. Here was a prophetic picture of His work in the Church, and of man's duty. His will is that the spiritual food of His Word and Sacraments should be supplied to the multitudes of Christendom, grouped together in Dioceses and Parishes.

This work of Christian organization was not performed in Ireland. In the age next to St. Patrick, and in the four following centuries, Ireland had many Teachers and Congregations, but it had no Parishes. It had a large number of Bishops ; but during the five hundred years of which we are now speaking, it had not a single Diocese [3].

Many circumstances impeded the development of

---

[1] The authorities for most of the statements made in this discourse may be found in the notes to the author's Occasional Sermons, Sermons xxvii. and xxviii. pp. 63—113, and therefore are not repeated here.

[2] πρασιαί. Mark vi. 40.

[3] Cp. Todd's St. Patrick, pp. 1. 3. 27. King's History, p. 146. King's Primacy of Armagh, p. 1. Thierry, "Histoire de la Conquête de l'Angleterre," p. 198.

the diocesan and parochial system in that country. The Celtic race, warm in its affections, generous in its aspirations, has been usually less patient of rule and order, and more prone to restlessness. The History of the Celtic Churches of Galatia, as seen in St. Paul's Epistle to them, exhibits a specimen of this characteristic temperament. Celtic enthusiasm, when moulded by Christian doctrine, and regulated by Apostolic discipline, produces noble results. Ireland gladly received the truths of the Gospel, but she did not enjoy the blessings of Apostolic discipline.

At that period, the country was occupied by numerous clans, under independent chiefs. St. Patrick had preached to some of those chiefs, and had converted them to Christianity; but his successors did not complete the work which he had begun. They did not prevail on these chiefs and their clans to coalesce in Christian unity; and many of these chiefs and clans relapsed into barbarism, and almost into paganism.

The Irish Bishops and clergy, not having appointed spheres of ministerial labour, and fearing the dangers incident to isolation in a wild country, formed themselves into ecclesiastical societies. Instead of adopting the diocesan and parochial system, the Church of Ireland developed itself in another form—the collegiate and monastic.

This latter system had many attractions, and produced some brilliant results. It made Ireland the University of the West. In the sixth and seventh centuries, young men were sent from our own and other lands to be trained in the Schools and Colleges of Ireland. The education which they there received, was a sound and scriptural one. Their teachers were distinguished by learning and holiness, and gained for Ireland the glorious title of the " Island of Saints."

These Collegiate Institutions were the nurseries of Christian missionaries. They sent forth St. Columba, born in the year of our Lord 521, of princely Irish blood, who founded the illustrious School of Iona.

The name of Iona itself is derived from St. Columba. It is called *I-colm-kill*, that is, the *Island of Columba* the founder of *churches*; for *kill*, you know, signifies a *church*, and the Latin *Columba*, a Dove, is, in its Hebrew equivalent, *Yona*, whence the name *Iona*; and the name of this small but famous isle of the West may not unfitly remind us, that many flocked to it, as the Prophet speaks, "like *doves to their windows* [4]" for spiritual peace and rest from the storms of the world; and fulfilled the prophecy, "*Surely the isles shall wait for Me;*" and many went forth from it on spiritual errands of peace and love, flying over the surging sea, like doves gleaming and glancing in the dark cloud, "covered with *silver wings and their feathers like gold* [5]."

Some who are here present have stood on the sea-girt cliffs of Iona, and have viewed with religious veneration the mouldering remains of ancient Christianity which survive on its solitary shore. The name of Iona has been justly coupled by a celebrated writer [6] with that of Marathon; but no laurels won on earthly fields can be compared with those which were gained by the soldiers of the Cross who went forth from Iona to advance the Kingdom of the Prince of Peace. St. Columba, the founder of the Missionary School of Iona, is commonly called the Apostle of the Highlands of Scotland and of the Western Isles. From Iona went forth St. Aidan, the Missionary Bishop of Northumberland and other northern regions of our own land, in the earlier part of the seventh century [7]. From Iona went

[4] Isa. lx. 8.   [5] Ps. lxviii. 13.
[6] Dr. Johnson, "Journey to the Western Islands of Scotland," p. 261. Edin. 1798. Cp. Wordsworth's Sonnets, vol. v. p. 238 :—
"To diffuse the WORD,
Her Temples rose 'mid pagan gloom ,—
Iona's Saints, forgetting not past days,
Garlands shall wear of amaranthine bloom,
While heaven's vast sea of voices chants their praise."
A.D. 635

forth St. Finan and St. Colman, who evangelized a
large part of central and southern England.

Ireland sent forth other Missionaries to the continent of Europe. At the head of these stands St.
Columbanus of Leinster, born about the middle of the
sixth century, who preached the Gospel in France and
Italy. Two Cantons of Switzerland, Glarus [8] and St.
Gall, still bear in their names the record of the zeal of
Irish Missionaries. St. Kilian went from Ireland to
preach Christ in Thuringia ; Virgilius, from the same
country, became Bishop of Saltzburg.

Let God's Name be blessed for these fruits of the
Holy Spirit, working in Ireland at that time.

But we must not be dazzled by these splendid results.
True it is, that in many parts of Ireland the light of
the Gospel was burning brightly. True it is, that
the candlesticks of other Churches were kindled from
it. But something more was wanted. The light was
burning with brilliant lustre within the Cloister and
the College, but it was not diffused with a healthful
radiance to the regions of Ireland around them. There
the light of the Gospel was waning. The shades of
barbarism and of paganism were falling thickly about
them.

We know what would be the condition of England,
if, instead of having a resident parochial Clergy, under
the vigilant eye of a Diocesan, our country were to
be left to the precarious ministrations of itinerant
preachers, issuing forth from the Colleges of our Uni-
versities, or from the precincts of our Cathedral
Churches.

Ireland was in that condition. She possessed many
learned and holy men in her religious houses ; she had
many wise teachers and zealous missionaries ; but
she had not a diocesan and parochial system. And
by reason of that defect, even at a time when Ireland

---

[8] So called from St. Hilarius, whose name was given to a church
dedicated by St. Fridolin, from Ireland ; St. Gall is so called from
St. Gallus, a scholar of St. Columbanus.

was called the "Island of Saints," and when she was
evangelizing other lands, her princes and people were
waging war with one another, and were lapsing into
unbelief*.

Here is a lesson for ourselves in our own missionary
work, at home and abroad.

Christian zeal profits little without Christian order.
The Christian Episcopate and Priesthood produce little
permanent good, in the work of Evangelization, unless
they move in the regular orbits of diocesan and parochial action. The Church of England will never be
able to perform her spiritual work at home in our
populous cities and country villages, until her Dioceses
are subdivided, and her Episcopate (which has only
received one addition for three hundred years) is increased according to the growth of her population,
and until her diocesan system is so proportioned and so
adjusted, that every child in her communion may be
able to feel, from personal experience, that he has a
Spiritual Father, a true Father in God.

The history of Ireland during this period may remind us also, that it is of little use to send forth missionaries to foreign lands, unless we plant regularly-
organized Churches; and that it is not enough to
extend the Church in the fulness of her threefold
ministry; but that threefold ministry must be enabled
to move and act in appointed spheres of labour, in
provinces, dioceses, and parishes.

For evidence of this truth, contemplate Ireland
during the period of which we are speaking. She had
zealous Missionaries, such as St. Columba, St. Columbanus, and many others: she was called the "Island
of Saints:" she was famous for her Colleges and
Schools. Let us not underrate the benefits derived
from these gifts of God; but still it cannot be denied,
that in the seventh, eighth, and ninth centuries her
condition was less hopeful spiritually, than it had been

* Cp. Todd, pp. 101. 107. 109. 122.

at the end of the fifth. And why? Because she did not imitate the pattern of Christ, who commanded His disciples to "make all the multitude sit down in companies on the green grass," in order that they might all be fed by Him, dispensing food to them by Apostolic hands. She did not follow the example of the ancient Churches of Christ. She did not walk according to their order and rule. She had Pastors without flocks; Bishops without Dioceses.

What, therefore, shall we say of those modern theories, which, instead of improving that diocesan and parochial system, which has now been established in Ireland however imperfectly, would break it down and shiver it to atoms, and would disintegrate and decompose the Church of Ireland into a promiscuous medley of incoherent congregations? Such a revolution as that would destroy the spiritual organization which exists in Ireland; and would bring back that disorder and anarchy which marred the work of evangelization there in early times, and brought with it a train of misery, civil as well as religious, of which we feel the effects at this day.

At the period of which we are speaking, Ireland, as we have said, had not adopted the diocesan and parochial system. She had many Bishops, but those Bishops had no Dioceses. Many of them lived in Collegiate and Monastic Institutions. The spiritual pre-eminence of these Bishops was acknowledged, but their Episcopal functions were exercised under the direction of the Heads of those Institutions.

We should have a parallel case in England, if our Bishops were drawn out of their Dioceses, and if the members of the Episcopate were absorbed into our Cathedrals and Colleges, and if their Episcopal ministrations, in ordaining and confirming, were to be placed under the control of the Deans of our Cathedrals, and of the Heads of our Colleges.

Monasticism domineered over Episcopacy in Ireland. And to such a degree did this anomaly prevail, that in some instances, where a woman was at the head of the Conventual Institution, the Bishop acted as her subaltern. This was the case at Kildare [1]. The Bishop of Kildare was the nominee and functionary of the Abbess St. Brigit and her successors.

May we not also here see a warning to ourselves? The foundation of Christian Institutions, in which women devote themselves to works of piety and charity, was sanctioned by Christian Antiquity, and may be hailed as a sign of spiritual life in our own day. But even for their own sakes, it is of paramount importance that these Christian Institutions should be well regulated. And is it not to be apprehended, that some of these Institutions are ready to make use of Episcopacy for their own purposes, so far as it does not interfere with their own organizations, and with the supremacy of their own head? Are there not some, who perhaps resemble St. Brigit in fame for sanctity, and are also not unlike her in love of power?

We may here make another application to ourselves.

Every one who loves God and His Church, must desire that the celebration of divine worship, which is the best preparation for the employment of heaven, and is the noblest work in which a society of men can be engaged, should be characterized by that uniform order, which bespeaks inward love, and by that simple grandeur, sober dignity, and chaste magnificence which we may call " the beauty of holiness."

But these epithets cannot be applied to those ritual innovations in public worship which are now growing up among us. And it deserves serious consideration, whether these practices may not be due to similar causes to those from which the evils of Ireland flowed —the present inadequacy of our diocesan system.

Wherever a Diocese is not too large, and wherever the voice of the Bishop may be heard throughout it, not speaking in the stern language of rigid •censure,

[1] Dr. Todd's St. Patrick, pp. 9, 10. 22—24, and King's History, p. 65.

but in the gentle accents of fatherly love ; wherever the Diocese is not too populous, and the Bishop can preside in person, in moderate-sized Diocesan Synods of Clergy and Laity, and take counsel with them ; and wherever the children of all the parishes of the Diocese, having been duly catechized by their pastors in their Christian faith and duty, are brought for Confirmation to the Bishop, and for admission to the Holy Communion ; and wherever the Bishop is able to visit personally all the parishes of his Diocese, and to administer confirmation to children,—not promiscuously by railfulls at once, in crowded congregations (as is now almost unavoidable from the size of our Dioceses and fewness of Bishops), but singly and solemnly, according to the rule of the Church, and in the quiet stillness of their own parish churches, in the presence of loving parents, sponsors, and friends,—there we may hope to see that all things will be " done decently and in order [2]," as is fitting in the house of God, and will tend to godly edification [3].

But, we can hardly venture to look for these blessed results in our own present condition.

The unwieldy size and vast populousness of our Dioceses, and the consequent feebleness of our diocesan and parochial system, forbid us to indulge that hope. And if remedies are not applied to these evils, we may expect to see, among other calamities, a further development of that private spirit, which is not content with the Book of Common Prayer, as settled by the joint sanctions of Church and State, and is not satisfied with those rites and ceremonies that are prescribed by lawful authority in the Church of England, but infringes order, and contravenes law, and breaks unity ; and (I say it with deep sorrow), while it professes a craving for a more catholic ritual, destroys that reverence for authority, and breaks those golden links of charity without which nothing profiteth [4], and which

---

[2] 1 Cor. xiv. 40.   [3] 1 Cor. xiv. 26.   [4] 1 Cor. xiii. 1.

are the very life of the Catholic Church; and therefore
cannot be said to be a truly catholic spirit, but rather
is selfish in its origin, sectarian in its character, and
schismatical in its practices[5], inasmuch as it rends
asunder the Church by divisions, and wastes her vital
energies, and exhausts her spiritual resources, and
paralyzes her efficiency; and recklessly casts stumbling-
blocks in the way of those immortal souls for which
Christ died; and is not spiritual, but sensuous[6], and
speaks to the eye rather than the heart; and takes
liberties with God's house, and treats it as if it were
its own abode, to be furnished according to its own
taste; and squanders in strifes about vestments and
postures that precious time, of which we shall have to
give an account at the Last Day to Christ, and which
ought to be used in saving the souls of those countless
myriads who are perishing around us; and tempts
men to spend their lives in profitless debates about the
"mint, anise, and cummin" of outward forms, rather
than in the godly exercise of "judgment, mercy, and
faith[7];" and excites riot and outrage, and may pro-
voke (it is to be feared) the intervention of the temporal Legislature, and paves the way for defections to
a corrupt faith and worship on one side, and for a
violent recoil to the blank and dreary baldness of a
chilling Puritanism on the other.

But to return. The Church of Ireland, having
Bishops but not Dioceses, and having adopted a monas-

---

[5] As Hooker observes, V. lxxi. 7. In all such matters as are
ceremonial "we make not our childish appeal, sometimes from
our own to foreign Churches, sometimes from both unto Churches
ancienter than both,—in effect, always from others to *ourselves*.
But, as becometh them that follow with all humility the way of
peace, we honour, reverence, and obey in very next degree unto
God, the voice of the *Church of God wherein we live."*
To obviate all misconstruction, the Author desires it to be
distinctly understood that the above paragraphs in the present
Sermon refer to practices which are *against* the *law* of the
English Church.

[6] Jude 19.   [7] Matt. xxiii. 23.

tic system rather than a parochial one, could not exercise a legitimate influence on the Laity. She reaped the fruits of her neglect, in the irreverent and sacrilegious acts of her princes and people. Even in the principal church of Ireland—that of Armagh—though the spiritual authority was nominally vested in a Bishop, or in two Bishops at once, yet the exercise of that spiritual authority was often controlled by a rude and illiterate chieftain, in whose hands the revenues were, and who claimed to be regarded as the representative of the founder of the church [8].

These chieftains of rival· clans were guilty of many excesses. They had little regard for holy things, and profaned and pillaged the houses of God. Ireland was distracted by intestine feuds. The temporal chiefs strove with one another [9]; and the secular power was not in harmony with the spiritual.

What were the consequences?

The Bishops became restless, and wandered forth into England and other countries, and endeavoured to exercise Episcopal functions in the Dioceses of those countries. Such acts were justly regarded as intrusive and irregular. These roving and vagrant Bishops from Ireland brought their office into contempt, and incurred the censure of English Synods in the ninth century [1].

---

[8] Dr. Todd's St. Patrick, pp. 155. 171, 172. 226. King's Primacy of Armagh, p. 2, folio, Armagh, 1854, in which volume is a valuable summary of early Irish Church History.

[9] Mr. King's History, p. 454.

[1] Especially the Synod of Cealcythe, A.D. 816. See Occasional Sermons, p. 64. Dr. Todd's St. Patrick, p. 40. Doubtless these censures were pronounced by persons and Councils under Roman influence; and the Church of Ireland, being independent of Rome, was an object of their antipathy. But she had laid herself open to them by her irregularities. They also incurred the rebuke of such men as Lanfranc and Anselm, Archbishops of Canterbury, in the eleventh century; and of St. Bernard, of Clairvaux. Lanfranc was Archbishop of Canterbury A.D. 1070—1093, Anselm 1093—1114. Lanfranc's censure may be seen in Abp. Ussher's Sylloge Epistolarum Hibernicarum, Nos. 26 and 27; Anselm's ibid. Nos. 33. 35, 36. See also Mr. King's History,

Weakened by internal division, Ireland and her Church became a prey to Danish and Norse invaders in the ninth century.   In course of time these Danish invaders were converted to Christianity.   But they refused to communicate with the ancient Church of Ireland.   Their sympathies were with the Norman princes and prelates of England, whose affections had been gained by the Church of Rome.   At that time the Bishops of Ireland, like the ancient Bishops of Britain, with whom they were on friendly relations, were independent of Rome.   In the eleventh century the Danish invaders imported from England into Ireland a rival Episcopate, which they set up in Dublin, and in some other maritime cities of Ireland.

Thus by means of England an avenue was made for the domination of the Church of Rome in Ireland. The Church of Rome was not slow to profit by that opening.   She nominated one of those Danish Bishops, whom England had ordained for Ireland, to be her own Legate in Ireland.   This was in the year of our Lord 1106.   That Bishop, Gillebert of Limerick, was the first Papal Legate there [2].   In the year 1151 Rome proceeded a step further.   In order to attach the leading Bishops of Ireland to her interests, she gave to four of that Episcopal body the titles of Archbishops, and sent to each of them the Pallium, which is her badge of the Archiepiscopal dignity; and without receiving which from her hands no Archbishop of her Communion is now permitted to exercise even Episcopal functions.   These four Irish Bishops accepted her gift: they looked to her for aid and protection against their own chieftains.   Here is a warning to temporal rulers and States.   Civil oppression of the Church produces ecclesiastical disaffection.   The spiritual domination of Hildebrand has no better ally than the worldly policy of Erastus.

pp. 423—433. St. Bernard's censure may be seen in his Vita Sancti Malachiæ (of Ireland), c. 10.

[2] Occasional Sermons, pp. 93. 127.

England first opened the way for Romish rule in Ireland. That work was completed by an English Pope, Nicholas Breakspeare, Hadrian IV., aided by an English king, Henry II. Hadrian IV., in a Papal brief, dated at Rome A.D. 1156, and directed to Henry, asserted that all Christian Islands belong to the Papacy[3]. On the ground of this claim, he gave Ireland to Henry, with the condition that he should levy Peter's pence yearly from every house in that land, to be paid to the Roman exchequer[4].

On the 17th October, 1171, Henry landed in Ireland, near Waterford, with 400 ships, and more than 4000 men; and many of the princes and prelates of Ireland, being divided among themselves, submitted to him; and in the following year, at the Council of Cashel, it was decreed that from that time the Church of Ireland should conform in public worship to that of England, which had then been brought into subjection to Rome. In the next year, 1173, Henry II. wrote these humiliating words to Pope Alexander III., in order to implore his aid against his own sons, "The realm of England is under thy jurisdiction; and, as regards feudal right, I am subject to thee alone[5]." That Pope rewarded his obsequiousness, by inditing three Papal briefs, in which he confirmed Henry's sovereignty over Ireland, on condition that he should hold it as tributary to Rome[6].

Thus Ireland became subject to England, and, through England, to Rome.

The calamities which have thence arisen, both to

[3] The Pontiff's words are, "Hiberniam et omnes insulas, quibus Sol justitiæ Christus illuxit, ad jus beati Petri et sacro-sanctæ Romanæ Ecclesiæ, non est dubium pertinere." The original is in Disputat. Apol. p. 8; cp. Ussher, Sylloge, p. 109, King's History, p. 1045.

[4] "De singulis ejus domibus annuam unius denarii beato Petro solvere pensionem."

[5] See Occasional Sermons, p. 110, for the original words.

[6] The originals may be seen ibid. p. 118. Cp. King, pp. 5. 1085—1090.

Ireland and England, are too many to recount here. England used the Papacy as her instrument for subjugating Ireland; and, by a remarkable retribution, Ireland has been used by the Papacy as its instrument against England. We owe much of our Christianity to Ireland; and Ireland owes her Romanism to us.

Let us briefly review what has now passed before us.

In the middle of the fifth century the Gospel of Christ was preached to Ireland by St. Patrick. The doctrine which he taught was the pure Word of God; the Church-government which he planted there was Apostolic. The faith of ancient Ireland was, as has been already shown, the same as that which is now professed by the united Church of England and Ireland[7].

This work, so happily begun, was not duly continued and perfected. Ireland was not portioned into Dioceses and Parishes. Her Teachers did not obey the command of Christ, "Make the men all sit down by companies upon the green grass." Her people were not fed from the hands of Christ by an Apostolic ministry in regular order. She had many Bishops, but no Dioceses. She had many Priests and congregations, but no Parishes. The Church developed herself in a Collegiate and Monastic form, not in the Diocesan and Parochial. The evil consequences of this mistake have been already considered. God chastened Ireland by intestine discord, and by foreign invasion, first by the Danes who pillaged and ravaged it, and set up a rival Church in it derived from England, and next by England herself, who subjugated it to Rome.

What shall we now say? At that time, the latter part of the twelfth century, when an English king was acknowledged for the first time as supreme in Ireland, England had a glorious opportunity of conferring inestimable benefits on Ireland, and on herself,

---

[7] See above, Sermon I., pp. 14—17.

and of obtaining a priceless reward from Christ, the King of kings, by promoting His glory, and by advancing His truth.

England was bound by ties of gratitude to do so. In earlier ages, the sixth and seventh centuries, Ireland, illustrious for her learning and her holiness, as the University of the West, and as the " Island of Saints," had educated many of the noblest and gentlest sons of Britain, and merited a grateful recompense at her hands. In the same centuries, Ireland, the Missionary School of the Western Isles of Scotland, and of England and Europe, had sent forth zealous and faithful preachers who had evangelized large portions of England. Ireland deserved a generous reward from England on this ground also.

In the eleventh century, Ireland was as yet free from the trammels of Rome. She had Bishops, but she had not Dioceses. England had Dioceses as well as Bishops, but she had bowed her neck beneath the Papal yoke.

What a glorious future of peace and prosperity then lay open to England and Ireland! They were united under one earthly king. Would to God that they had also been joined together in truth and love under the same heavenly Lord, Jesus Christ! What blessings would then have accrued to both, if England had not only communicated to Ireland her diocesan and parochial system (this, indeed, God be thanked, she did*), but if she had not blemished and marred that gift by enforcing the Papal Supremacy in Ireland; and if she had preserved to Ireland her ancient spiritual freedom, and had followed the example of that spiritual independence, and had learnt the lessons which are taught by the history of Ireland, and by the time-honoured names of St. Patrick, St. Columba, St. Columbanus, and others, that a land may be the " Land of Saints," and a Church may be an University of Europe, and a Seminary

---

* About A.D. 1110, at the Synod of Rathbreasail, an arrangement was made for the first time for the division of Ireland into Dioceses. King's Primacy of Armagh, p. 1 : cp. History, p. 451.

D

of Christian Missionaries, without being subject to
Rome, or even in communion with her, and without
any other Head but Christ [9].

That lesson was not learnt by England in the twelfth
century. That glorious opportunity was lost. But,
God be thanked, it is now offered to us again in the
nineteenth century; perhaps for the last time. Shall
we not rejoice to embrace it? Brethren, we owe much
to Ireland. The Gospel was preached in England and
Scotland by Irish Missionaries more than a thousand
years ago. Many generations of our forefathers were
brought to Christ, and to life eternal in Him, by those
Irish Missionaries, and will acknowledge them with
gratitude and love as their spiritual fathers, at the Last
Day. What return shall we make to the Church of
Ireland for those benefits? Shall we be so unthankful
and so ungenerous, as to requite her with sacrilegious
spoliation? Heaven forbid! Shall we not rather endeavour to promote the pure Gospel there, which we
received at her hands? Shall we not rejoice to reward
her for spiritual blessings derived from her, and to in-
demnify her for spiritual wrongs inflicted upon her?

Let us not be cheated by the delusive assertion,
which betrays the grossest ignorance of history, and is
not creditable to those who propagate it, that Romanism is "the ancient religion of Ireland," and that
they who renounce the errors of Romanism in Ireland,
and join the communion of the national Church, "abjure
the faith of their fathers and embrace a new Religion."

Brethren, as we have shown, the very reverse is the
case. The faith of the Church of Ireland is the ancient
faith of Ireland. Romanism is a new religion. It
came in by stealth into Ireland in an age of darkness.

The Bishop of Rome exercised no authority in Ireland for a thousand years after Christ. I make this
assertion solemnly in the presence of Almighty God.

[9] No Saint of Ireland—the "Island of Saints"—was canonized
by Rome before St. Malachias, A.D. 1190.

Those persons who renounce the errors and corruptions
of Rome, and communicate with the Church of Ireland,
return to the "old faith of the ancient Church of Ireland [1]."

Our English and Norman forefathers, who introduced
Romanism into Ireland in the twelfth century, did not
enjoy the pure light of the Gospel, which is now diffused among us. They had not the free access to the
Scriptures that we have in the nineteenth century.
They lived in a time of spiritual gloom, and were deceived by forged documents—such as the Papal decre-
tals—and by false pretences, such as those of Pope
Hadrian's brief. We have no such excuse. Our re-

---

[1] Those persons who have been induced to speak of Romanism
as the "old creed," the "ancient religion," of Ireland, are invited
to examine carefully and to consider seriously the following historical facts:—

1. The Bishops and Clergy of Ireland, for a thousand years after
Christ, took no oath of subjection to the Pope.

2. They did not resort to Rome for bulls of investiture.

3. They did not appeal to Rome for the determination of
Ecclesiastical causes.

4. The Bishops of Ireland were not appointed by the Pope, but
by nomination of the chieftains, or by election of the Clergy.

5. The Church of Ireland, for a thousand years after Christ,
was independent of Rome; and in the eleventh and twelfth centuries was even denounced by Popes and Romish writers as schismatical.

6. No Papal Legate was ever known in Ireland before the
twelfth century.

7. No Archiepiscopal Pall was ever received in Ireland from
Rome before the twelfth century.

These facts are sufficient to prove that the Papal supremacy
was never acknowledged in Ireland in ancient times. And the
Papal supremacy is the keystone of Romanism; it is, according
to Cardinal Bellarmine and the most celebrated Romish writers,
the essence of the Christian religion; and whosoever does not
acknowledge it, is denounced by Rome as a heretic, and without
hope of salvation. From these and other evidences it is clearly
manifest, that Romanism was not the ancient religion of Ireland;
and it is no less certain, that the religion now professed by the
National Church was, in all essentials, the ancient religion of
Ireland.

sponsibilities therefore are far greater than theirs. We know that the Papal Supremacy rests on no sure foundation of Scripture and primitive Antiquity. It is a tree which our Heavenly Father hath not planted, and which will one day be rooted up [2], and will be withered, like the barren fig-tree, by the breath of Christ.

Let us not be so infatuated as to reduce the Church of Ireland to that disorganization which made it an easy prey to Roman ambition, and which brought upon it and upon us a flood of evils. Let us not dissolve the Church into a confused chaos of dislocated congregations. Rather let us unite with her in zealous endeavours to cherish, extend, and strengthen her diocesan and parochial system. Let us earnestly labour, and fervently pray, that the weary multitudes of the whole population of Ireland may be made to sit down, in well-ordered and loving companies, on the green grass of Christ's holy Catholic Church, and that they may there be fed, not with the withered husks of legendary fables and heretical dogmas, but with the healthful food of Christ's holy Word and Sacraments, blessed and supplied by Him who is the Living Bread that came down from Heaven [3], and dispensed by the ministry of Apostolic hands, so that all may be filled. And may we, being united with them, in feeding on that heavenly food, be admitted hereafter to see Christ face to face, and through His infinite merits, and most powerful mediation, may we with them be accepted as His own, and be invited by Him to sit down together with them, and with all the Saints in glory, in the Kingdom of God!

[2] Matt. xv. 13.   [3] John vi. 33. 50, 51.

SERMON III.

ACTS vii. 26.

"Sirs, ye are brethren; why do ye wrong one to another?"

AT the close of the last Discourse on the history of
Christianity in Ireland, we were brought to a critical
era in the annals of that country.

In the year of our Lord 1171, the Church of Ireland,
which till that time owned no other Head than Jesus
Christ, was brought, by means of England, into sub-
jection to the Church of Rome. Ireland submitted to
Henry II., King of England, which was under the
Roman Papacy, then at the zenith of its power.

From that time, and during four hundred years,
until the Reformation, in the sixteenth century, Ireland
had a Roman Catholic religious establishment.

A Roman Catholic Church establishment in Ireland
is regarded by some persons as a remedy for the evils
of that country. The majority of the population of
Ireland is now Roman Catholic, and therefore it is
argued that, as an act of justice and expediency, the
Roman Catholic religion ought to be established there.

If the question of religious establishments were one
which is to be determined solely by reference to tables
of population (which, doubtless, are not to be neglected),
this conclusion could not be gainsaid.

But what do we here learn from the Word of God?

In the days of Ahab, King of Israel, the prophet
Elijah stood on Mount Carmel and said, "I, even I
only, remain, a prophet of the Lord; but Baal's prophets are four hundred and fifty men [1]." Elijah was
there alone, and they had the King, the Queen, and
the people on their side; but Elijah did not therefore
deem that the worship of Baal ought to be made the
national religion of Israel. No: his language to the
people was, "If the Lord be God, follow Him; but if
Baal, then follow him [2]."

There may be therefore other elements which enter
into this problem, besides that of numerical majorities;
and which may outweigh the considerations derivable
from such majorities.

Let us apply this principle to the case before us—
that of Ireland.

It ought to be inquired, calmly and dispassionately,
whether there are not some elements in Romanism
which disqualify it from being a national religious
establishment, especially in a country like our own,
where the chief power is vested in one of a different
faith.

The Church of Rome at the present day, by her
worship of the Blessed Virgin, and (to adopt her own
term) by her *adoration* [3] of the Roman Pontiff, is
undermining the religion and worship of Jesus Christ;
which is the surest foundation of Governments, and
the best safeguard of the peace and prosperity of states,
and of the true liberty of nations.

The Church of Rome,—by strange superstitions
and religious impostures,—is revolting the intelligence
of the Laity in Roman Catholic countries from Christianity itself, which they identify with Romanism—

---

[1] 1 Kings xviii. 22.   [2] 1 Kings xviii. 21.

[3] "Adoratio Pontificis" is the language of the Roman Ceremonial, and "Quem creant, adorant" is the language of Roman
coins; and it pervades the doctrine of her schools, and is a fundamental principle of her theology, as may be seen in the evidence
adduced by the Author in his note on Rev. xvii. 14, p. 234.

being the only form of Christianity with which they are acquainted—and is thus preparing a triumph for Infidelity; which—unless God in His mercy restrain it—will burst forth with antichristian fury, in civil anarchy and social confusion, and will sweep with a fierce hurricane and terrible tornado over Europe, and produce ruin and desolation.

The Church of Rome lays claim to spiritual supremacy, domineering over all other power in a nation, and establishing an empire of her own, paramount to all other authority. She brings that supremacy to bear, with mysterious energy, on every social relation of life. By means of her Confessional, and by her theory of the non-obligation of Oaths, if prejudicial to her interest (of which she is to be the judge), and by her assertion of power to absolve from their obligation, she wields an irresistible sway over the conscience. She can arm subjects against rulers (as has been recently seen in Italy), and soldiers against their sovereigns [4]. By means of the Oath [5] which she imposes on every Bishop in her communion, requiring them "to maintain the royalties of St. Peter"—that is, the claims of the Roman Papacy—" against all men," and, " to persecute and to wage war against all heretics and schismatics" (that is, all who will not bow down to her), she has rendered her system almost intolerable even in Roman Catholic states, and how much more in Protestant countries!

By such principles as these, the Church of Rome has disqualified herself from being accepted as the religious instructress of nations; especially of a people subject to a Protestant throne, like our own, which she denounces and anathematizes as heretical and schismatic. And the larger the population is, which is committed

---

[4] The Author has given, in another place, abundant evidence of the truth of these statements; and if they are challenged, he holds himself in readiness to reproduce it.

[5] The oath may be seen in the "Pontificale Romanum," printed by authority at Rome, p. 62, ed 1818.

to her influence, the more danger will be incurred by those who strengthen that influence, by accepting the Church of Rome as the national teacher of religion.

If therefore Romanism is not accepted by the United Kingdom of Great Britain and Ireland as the national religion in Ireland, the Church of Rome ought not to ascribe that non-acceptance to any sectarian antipathies on our part, but simply and solely to her own avowed principles.

Brethren, it is devoutly to be wished that all Churches were joined together in one. Let us all labour and pray for unity : but let it be for unity in the Truth. Unity in error is conspiracy against Truth. It is treachery to Christ, Who is the Truth[6], and Who came to bear witness to the Truth, and Who prayed for His disciples that they might be sanctified in the Truth.

This being the case, if we would cleave to Christ and to the Truth, we cannot be united with the Church of Rome. She has made such union impossible. She has added novel and erroneous dogmas to the ancient Faith of the Christian Church. She claims supremacy over all other Churches, and she makes communion in her errors to be essential to communion with herself. And by pretending to be infallible, she has enthralled herself in the perpetual bondage of maintaining her errors, instead of renouncing them ; and would involve others, who unite with her, in the same necessity of erring.

Some indeed there are, even among ourselves, who endeavour to harmonize the creed of Rome with the faith of the Church of England and of the Primitive Church. But such accommodations will never approve themselves to men of clear judgments and honest hearts. And why ? Because the question between England and Rome is not one of details, but of principle. It is not one of superstructure merely, but of foundations.

[6] John xiv. 16; xvii. 17; xviii. 37.

It is not, whether such or such decrees of the Council of Trent may or not be reconciled, by an ingenious process of adjustment, with such or such Articles of the Church of England. But the real question at issue is, —whether the two Churches of England and Rome are not built on two totally different and opposite foundations.

The Church of England,—following the Primitive Church [7], — affirms that Holy Scripture contains all things necessary to salvation [8], and that nothing is to be required of any man to be believed as an article of Faith, which is not read in Scripture, or may not be proved thereby. The Church of England affirms the supremacy and the sufficiency of Holy Scripture. She builds her faith on this foundation, and on it alone. She builds her house on a Rock—the Rock of God's holy Word.

But the Church of Rome does not build her faith on this foundation. She asserts [9] that Scripture is *not* sufficient, and is *not* supreme; she affirms that Scripture requires to be eked out by unwritten traditions, of which she professes to be the depository; and which, she says, ought to be received with the same veneration as the written Word of God. And from her stock of unwritten traditions she brings out, from time to time, new and unscriptural dogmas, such as those which she added in the Trent Creed to the ancient faith of the Church, and · such as the dogma of the Immaculate

---

[7] As Hooker says (II. v. 3), "To urge any thing as part of that supernatural and celestially revealed truth which God hath taught, and *not to show it in Scripture,* this did the Ancient Fathers evermore think unlawful, impious, execrable:" cp. Hooker II. viii. 7.

[8] In her Sixth Article.

[9] In the Fourth Session of the Council of Trent (A.D. 1546), which she asserts to have been infallible, and inspired by the Holy Ghost. And therefore the most eminent Romish Theologians expressly reject the notion (sometimes charitably imputed to them) that the Church of Rome builds her faith on Scripture only. See Cardinal Bellarmine, De Verbo Dei iv. 12. Perrone, De Locis Theolog. pt. ii. sect. ii.

Conception, which she promulgated the other day, and
which she requires to be received by all as necessary to
salvation. And thus she incurs the anathema pronounced by Jesus Christ Himself against those who
make " the Word of God of none effect by their traditions," and who "teach for doctrines the command-
ments of men [1]."

It is therefore mere idle trifling, yea, it is a dan-
gerous delusion, to compare such or such specific Articles
of the Church of England with such or such decrees of
the Council of Trent, and, after dexterous manipulations
of them, to represent that they are not repugnant to
each other, and that therefore the Church of England
may safely coalesce with the Church of Rome. This
is as if a surveyor or architect should report to us that
two or three rooms in one house correspond in dimen-
sions of feet and inches with two or three rooms in
another, and that therefore both houses are equally safe
for us to dwell in. Brethren, what are measurements
of rooms to us, when we want to know about the foundations? An idle mockery. Let those reconcilers of
opposite systems of Churches not talk to us of rooms,
but let them be desired to report to us on foundations.

Brethren, with such light as God has given me, I
have endeavoured long and carefully to examine the
foundation of the two Churches, and this is my report
to you thereon. The Church of England is built on a
sound foundation, because it is built on the Written
Word of God. Therefore you may safely dwell in it.
The Church of Rome is not built on a sound foundation, because it is not built on that Word. Therefore
you may not dwell in it. The one is built on a rock,
the other is built on the sand. And if we join ourselves to Rome as she is, then, when the storm comes,
and the winds blow, and beat violently upon that
house, and it falls [2], then we also shall fall with it—
and great will be the fall thereof.

<hr>

[1] Matt. xv. 6. 9.   [2] Matt. vii. 24—28.

But while we are forced to affirm, that union with the Church of Rome, as she is, is not possible for those who do not desire to be separated from Christ; yet we should be deeply grieved to suppose, that there are not many good men, both Clergy and Laity, amongst Roman Catholics of Ireland, who would be disposed to unite with us on the solid basis of Holy Scripture, as interpreted by the consent and practice of the Primitive Church.

Why should not Roman Catholic Bishops and Priests in Ireland be invited to meet the Bishops and Clergy of the national Church in friendly conference, and to consider the grounds of their differences, and endeavour to heal their divisions? There is ample room in Ireland for the zeal and energy of both. Let them unite together in preaching the Gospel of Christ, as it was preached fourteen centuries ago by St. Patrick, the Apostle of Ireland; and then we shall heartily rejoice, —more than words can express,—to be joined together with them in winning souls to Christ.

But further, this question concerning a Roman Catholic Church establishment in Ireland, ought not to be argued merely on *à priori* grounds.

The fact is, the experiment has been already tried. The Roman Catholic Church *was* established in Ireland for almost four centuries, namely, from near the close of the twelfth century until the Reformation in the sixteenth century. We can therefore appeal to experience.

What were its results?

If the Church of Rome is indeed, as she calls [3] herself, "the Mother and Mistress of Churches;" if her candlestick is the spiritual luminary of Christendom; if the Roman Pontiff is indeed the Vicar of Christ, Who is the Light of the World and the Prince of Peace; if these assertions are true, then that period of four hundred years, in which Rome was the estab-

[3] In the Trent Creed.

lished Church of Ireland, ought to have been one of
spiritual and intellectual illumination.

But was this the case? Assuredly not. That
period was one of thick spiritual darkness.

Before that time (as we have already seen [4]) Ireland
had been called the Island of Saints; she had been the
University of the West; she had been the Seminary
of Christian Missions to Scotland, England, and the
continent of Europe. But *after* that date Ireland was
under an eclipse.

In inquiring what were the fruits of a Roman
Catholic Church establishment in Ireland in the four
hundred years between the twelfth and sixteenth centuries, we need not dwell on the rapacious extortion
and exactions of Roman Legates in Ireland; nor on the
collations by Rome of Irish Bishoprics and other dig-
nities on Italians, sometimes on boys and absentees [5];
nor on the vast treasure drawn out of Ireland to Rome
at that time. Let us pass by these and proceed to
other evidence.

In the history of that period,—the twelfth to the
sixteenth century,—there are two remarkable public
documents, which exhibit in clear light the effects of
the Roman Catholic Church establishment in Ireland
at that period.

(1.) The first of these is a petition and remonstrance
of the Roman Catholic nobles of Ireland to the Bishop
of Rome, Pope John XXII., in the reign of King
Edward II., in the year 1318 [6].

This was not an address of Protestants, but of
Roman Catholics, and it was sent to their spiritual
head, the Bishop of Rome.

---

[4] See above, pp. 21—23.

[5] See the evidence of this in the notes on Occas. Sermons
already quoted, pp. 132—135, and p. 183.

[6] Large extracts from the original document may be seen in
Occas. Sermons, pp. 150—152. An English translation of it is
given in King's History, pp. 1119—1135, and there is a sketch of
its contents in Dr. Todd's St. Patrick, p. 237.

In it the petitioners complain that Pope Hadrian IV., being an Englishman, and swayed by English partialities, and deceived by English misrepresentations, had given Ireland to England, and that Ireland had been plundered by English settlers, who had invaded it under pretence of zeal for religion. They affirm that piety and virtue have suffered grievous injury from them : that Irish Bishops and Prelates were arrested and imprisoned by the ministers of the King of England in Ireland. They complain that in the administration of law, invidious distinctions are made between the English colonists and Irish natives ; that if an Englishman kills an Irishman, no penalty is inflicted on the murderer; and that the murderer is treated with honour by the English, even by English Bishops (who, be it remembered, were nominated or approved by Rome), and that it is a doctrine publicly taught by those English ecclesiastics in Ireland (who were all Roman Catholic prelates), that it is no greater crime to kill an Irishman than it is to kill a dog, and that no one of Irish blood ought to be received as a member of any English religious house in Ireland ; that in consequence of these rigorous enactments and cruel outrages, civil feuds have raged in Ireland since the grant of Ireland to England by the Pope, and that during that period 50,000 persons have been murdered by the sword, and many others have been destroyed by famine, and have perished in prisons. They conclude their remonstrance to the Pope by saying that their patience has been exhausted by English injustice and tyranny, and that they have chosen for themselves another king, Edward Bruce, brother of Robert Bruce, King of Scotland, in place of the English sovereign, and they request the Roman Pontiff to sanction their choice, and to restrain the King of England from further oppression of Ireland.

The question here is, Did the Bishop of Rome, the spiritual Head of the Church of Ireland, intervene to redress these grievances? Did he mediate between

the two parties, both of which were Roman Catholics
and acknowledged his supremacy? Did he say to
them, like the Hebrew leader of old, "Sirs, ye are
brethren; why do ye wrong one to another?" No;
on the contrary, the use which he made of his power
is sufficiently evident from the second of the two
documents already mentioned.

(2.) This second document is a celebrated statute,
called "the Statute of Kilkenny," made by English
Roman Catholic Bishops, nobles, and others in the
Parliament of Ireland, in A.D. 1367, about half a century after the petition of the Irish Roman Catholic
nobles and others just described.

In this statute it was enacted that no Irishman
should be received into any ecclesiastical benefice or
religious house among the English in Ireland; that
no Irishman, resident among the English there, should
be allowed to use the Irish language, his own native
tongue; Irish laws and customs were proscribed.
Intermarriages of the English with the Irish were
forbidden. Englishmen were not permitted to allow
the cattle of Irishmen to graze on their lands. In a
word, the tendency of this statute was to perpetuate
the hatred between the Irish Roman Catholics and
the English Roman Catholics in Ireland.

What, again let us ask, did the Bishop of Rome do?
Did he endeavour to pacify them? Did he rise up in
his seat of authority and say, "Sirs, ye are brethren;
why do ye wrong one to another?" No, he did not.
On the contrary, the Roman Catholic Bishops of
Ireland, who were most of them nominees of the Pope,
accepted this unchristian statute, and many of them
pledged themselves to denounce sentence of excom-
munication on those who violated it [7].

Such were the results of a Roman Catholic establishment in Ireland. Romanism did not allay these dis-

[7] Cp. Todd, pp. 235, 236. King, pp. 661. 1139—1148. Large
extracts from the Statute itself may be seen in Occas. Sermons,
pp. 152, 153.

cords. Rather it fomented them. It ruled by dividing its own subjects against each other. It was strong by their weaknesses. Under the supremacy of the Bishop of Rome, who claims to be the Vicar of Christ, and the Representative of the Prince of Peace, the Roman Catholic English in Ireland were arrayed in deadly antagonism against the Roman Catholic Irish in Ireland. The bitter fruits of this war of race against race remain to this day.

Wherefore, brethren, do we recount these things? Not, God knows, for the sake of reviving painful recollections of national animosities. Heaven forbid! But to guard against false hopes and vain illusions; to prevent aggravations of existing evils by the application of remedies which would only inflame the disease; to render justice to Ireland; to defend the cause of God and His truth.

The calamities of Ireland are *not* due to repugnance on her part to receive the Gospel of Christ. No; as we have already seen [8], she readily accepted the Word of God when preached to her, fourteen hundred years ago, by St. Patrick the Apostle of Ireland. The Celtic population of Ireland welcomed the Apostle of Ireland with generous enthusiasm, as the Celtic population of Galatia welcomed St. Paul, for whom they would have given their eyes in grateful return for the spiritual light of the Gospel [9]. St. Patrick won their affections by preaching to them in their own tongue, and he conciliated the chieftains of Ireland by addressing himself first to them, and by enlisting their sympathies in the cause of the Gospel, and by Christianizing their clans through them, by means of a native ministry raised from the families of the chiefs.

The calamities of Ireland are *not* due to any aversion on her part to the Holy Scriptures, and to the true Catholic faith, and to primitive Apostolic discipline, free from Roman additions. She received

---

[8] See above, pp. 7, 8. 13—17.   [9] Gal. iv. 15.

the Holy Scriptures in ancient times. She received
the Creed of St. Patrick, untainted by Romish ad-
mixtures. She received Apostolic Church Government, and knew nothing of Romish Supremacy.

Yet, further, the miseries of Ireland do *not* arise
from any love on her part for that Supremacy, as
such. From the age of St. Patrick to the eleventh
century, the Church of Ireland was independent of
Rome [1]. And in the next four hundred years,
during which she had experience of Romish Supremacy, she suffered so much evil from its influence that
in the 16th century, in the year 1537, she readily
renounced that supremacy, and her chieftains submitted even to Henry VIII., although he was then
excommunicated by Rome [2]. And in the reign of his
son, Edward VI., and of his daughter, Queen Elizabeth,
the Reformation was accepted with scarcely a dis-
sentient voice by the whole Irish Episcopate [3].

But, if the truth must be spoken, the calamities of
Ireland are due, in great measure, to England. They
are due to the ambition, covetousness, and tyranny of
English Princes, Prelates, and nobles; a tyranny
sanctioned by the Roman Papacy, and continued
under its influence for four hundred years.

These sins of our forefathers exasperated Ireland
against England. They produced national antipathy;
they kindled a war of race against race. They drove
Ireland to take refuge under the Roman Papacy and
to invoke its aid against England. And thus England,
which had introduced the Papacy into Ireland, was
scourged by the Papacy, which she had used for her
own aggrandizement. By the sins of England herself, Ireland has now become " England's difficulty."
And the reason why the Reformation was not accepted
by the body of the Irish People was, because, where it

---

[1] See Sermons, pp. 43—45. 63—65. 127.
[2] See the evidence in the Sermons above quoted, pp. 187—197.
[3] See ibid. pp. 208—217.

was presented to them at all, it was *not* presented to
them in an Irish dress, but in an English. It came to
them in the garb and with the gait of an invader and
a conqueror, speaking stern words in a strange language, and not in the loved accents of their native
tongue.

At the time of the Reformation, the native language
of Ireland was proscribed by English rule in that
country, as if the Irish tongue was unfit for the service
of God. In defiance of a fundamental principle of the
Reformation that "it[4] is a thing plainly repugnant
to the Word of God, and to the custom of the Primitive Church to have public prayer in the Church, or
to minister the sacraments, in a tongue not under-
standed of the people:" it was enacted[5] by English
authority in Ireland, in the year 1560, that "where the
minister of an Irish Parish did not understand English
he might say the Common Prayer—not in Irish, but
in the *Latin* tongue."

Yet, further. The wise and charitable plans which
were afterwards devised by the Irish Convocation of
the Clergy in 1703 and 1711 for disseminating the
Scriptures in the Irish language, and for raising up an
Irish-speaking Ministry in Ireland, were thwarted and
overruled by the temporal power and influence of
England, as destructive to what was called "the
English interest in Ireland[6]."

England then ruled in Ireland; but not a single
copy of the New Testament was printed in the Irish
language at the Reformation: the first edition of it
appeared in 1603. Not a single copy of the Old
Testament was printed in the Irish language at the
Reformation; no edition of it appeared till the year

[4] Thirty-nine Articles, Art. XXIV.
[5] In the Act of Uniformity for Ireland.
[6] See Bishop Mant's History of the Irish Church, ii. 164.
Occasional Sermons, pp. 249, 285, and the paper of the Rev.
Dr. Butcher (now Lord Bishop of Meath) read at the Norwich
Congress in 1865, "On the position of the Church in Ireland,"
p. 13.

E

1686. Only 1250 copies of the New Testament were printed in Irish in the whole of the 17th century, and only 500 copies of the Old Testament. Not a single copy of the Book of Common Prayer was printed in Irish at the Reformation, nor till the year 1608. And what was still worse, in the whole of the 18th century not a single copy of the Old or New Testament was printed in the Irish tongue [7]. England, Protestant England, protested against Protestantism; and countenanced Romanism. England, Protestant England, for her own selfish purposes of temporal policy and worldly aggrandizement, contravened the principles of the Reformation, and imitated the practices of Rome. She denied to the Irish the Scriptures and Common Prayer in their own tongue.

The wrongs that had been inflicted on Ireland by Roman Catholic England during the four hundred years before the Reformation still rankled and festered in the hearts of the Irish. The soothing balm of Christianity, speaking to them in its own soft tones in their mother tongue, was not applied to allay them. On the contrary, many laws were enacted by English rule which embittered those animosities. The ancient clanships of Ireland were broken down, the chieftains were impoverished and exasperated [8]. Many of them fled to foreign lands, and connected themselves with foreign and Papal powers, hostile to England, in hopes of recovering their property and of expelling the English colonists. Irish laws were abolished, and English laws were not established in their place. The peasantry were left without the guidance of their ancient chiefs, and became the victims of foreign intrigue [9].

The Bishop of Rome was not slow to avail himself of this national hostility to England, which had then

[7] Cp. the details in Occasional Sermons, pp. 248—250. 285.
[8] Cp. Todd's St. Patrick, pp. 226—230.
[9] Cp. Phelan's "Policy of the Church of Rome in Ireland," p. 141.

thrown off his yoke. He practised on the disaffection of the chieftains and people of Ireland, exasperated against England; he excommunicated and denounced[1] the sovereigns of England in the years 1570, 1580, 1587, 1600, 1606, 1626, and excited the chieftains and people of Ireland to rise up in revolt 'against them[2], and promised blessings temporal and eternal for rebellion. He introduced into Ireland a new Episcopate from Italy and Spain[3], and thus rent the Irish Church by a schism which has not been healed to this day. The violence and fury of wrath and revenge which were thus inflamed, may be inferred from such language as the following, which can hardly be quoted without a shudder, and may be seen in a book published under Romish authority in the year 1645[4]: "Ye men of Ireland, proceed onward on your course, and complete the work of your liberation! Destroy your heretical enemies! Ye have already slain 150,000 of them in the four or five years that are past, as your adversaries themselves allow. Would to God ye had slain them all!"

How different is such language as this from that of him who said, ".Sirs, ye are brethren; why do ye wrong one to another?"

What, therefore, shall we now say? Surely it is an error to say, with some, that "Ireland has rejected the Reformation;" and that "the Reformation has failed in Ireland."

Such language is a slander and calumny against Ireland; it is an affront to Almighty God. For what was

---

[1] See the details in Occasional Sermons, p. 243.
[2] See ibid. pp. 204. 228. 242. 244, 245.
[3] Ibid. p. 227. Cp. King's History, pp. 889—914.
[4] Disputatio Apologetica de jure regni Hiberniæ pro Catholicis Hibernis adversus hæreticos Anglos. Francofurti, Superiorum permissu, Anno Domini 1645, p. 125. The book is very scarce. The avowed design of the Author is to stir up the Irish to exterminate the English from Ireland, and to recover the confiscated lands of that country, from the hands of English proprietors, to their ancient Irish possessors.

the Reformation ? The English Reformation made no
new Bible ; it created no new Creed ; it instituted no
new Sacraments ; it formed no new Church ; it set up
no new Altar ; it invented no new Order of Ministry.
No ; it preserved and restored the old. The Reformers
themselves were frail and erring men : and some, who
called themselves reformers, were guilty of heinous
sins. But the Reformation itself was of God; and to
say that the Reformation has been rejected by Ireland,
is to say that Ireland has rejected God ; to say that
the Reformation has failed in Ireland, is to say that
He has failed there.

But what is the fact ?

It is, that the Reformation has never been fairly
offered to Ireland. It has not been rejected ; for it
has not been duly presented there. This is clear from
the facts already laid before you. If the Reformation
had been offered to Ireland, as St. Patrick would have
offered it, and as he did offer the Gospel to Ireland in
the fifth century ;—if it had come to them in the
native language of Ireland ; if it had addressed itself
to the chieftains of Ireland after St. Patrick's example ;
if it had endeavoured to win the clans of Ireland by
means of their chiefs ; if it had raised up, as he did, a
native Episcopate and Priesthood in Ireland from the
families of these chiefs, and if England had not too
often abused her Church-patronage by bestowing the
best Bishoprics and benefices in Ireland on English
strangers, knowing nothing of the Irish language, and
caring little for the Irish people, and recommended
mainly by servile sycophancy to English statesmen,
reckless of Christ's prerogatives, and thinking only of
things that perish ; and if Ireland had then spurned it
from her, then indeed it might be said that the Reformation had been rejected in Ireland,—but not otherwise.

The enthusiastic joy with which the Gospel was
received by Ireland in the fifth century is a proof
of the welcome—aye, the ecstasy and rapture—with
which the same Gospel would have been hailed in the

sixteenth century, if it had been offered to Ireland in the same manner.

The Reformation has not failed in Ireland.   No, brethren; but we, ourselves, both before the Reformation, and during the Reformation, and after the Reformation, have failed, miserably failed, and are now failing in our duty to God and to His Church, to the Reformation and to Ireland herself.   Our sins have found us out, and He has punished us thereby.   Let us not charge God with the consequence of our own sins. Let us not impute our own failures to Him and His holy Word.   Let us not ascribe to the Reformation the faults of those who enjoyed the light of the Reformation and yet sinned against it.   Let us not accuse Ireland, when we ourselves are guilty in His sight. Let us not arraign, punish, and pillage the Church in Ireland, for shortcomings, blemishes, and weaknesses which are the results of the wrongs which we ourselves have inflicted upon her. ·No : heaven forbid! but let us acknowledge God's righteous retribution, and let us learn wisdom from the past.   Let us not indulge in mutual recriminations and in uncharitable invectives, but let us pray especially for our Roman Catholic brethren in Ireland, whose differences from us are due in great measure to our own lack of zeal and faithfulness.   Let us humble ourselves before God, and say: " Righteous and true are Thy judgments, Thou King of Nations, who shall not fear Thee⁵?"   " O Lord, righteousness belongeth unto Thee, but unto us confusion of face, to our kings, to our princes, and to our fathers. We have sinned against Thee.   O God, incline Thine ear and hear, open Thine eyes and behold our desolations, for Thy city and Thy people are called by Thy name⁶."   " Remember not, Lord, our iniquities, nor the iniquities of our forefathers, neither take Thou vengeance of our sins."

⁵ Jer. x. 7.   Rev. xv. 3; xvi. 7; xix. 2.
⁶ Dan. ix. 8, 9. 18, 19.

"Let us be watchful and strengthen the things that remain[7]." "Let us speak the truth in love[8]." Let us cherish more and more the spirit of the Gospel of truth and peace in our own hearts, and labour and pray that its voice may be heard by every ear and sink into every heart in Ireland; for the Gospel, and the Gospel alone, can heal our wounds and hers: the Gospel and the Gospel alone can speak with a voice of power, as well as of love, and say,—

"Sirs, ye are brethren; why do ye wrong one to another?"

[7] Rev. iii. 2.   [8] Eph. iv. 14.

SERMON IV.

ON THE CHURCH OF IRELAND AS A NATIONAL
RELIGIOUS ESTABLISHMENT.

JOHN vii. 24.

" Judge not according to the appearance, but judge righteous
judgment."

AFTER reviewing, in previous discourses, the history of
Christianity in Ireland, we are now brought to the following question, viz. :—

Ought the Church of Ireland to be maintained as
the religious Establishment of that country ?

The question is *not*—

Whether any other form of religion should be
established in its place. The most powerful adversaries of the Church in Ireland, who have now
made an alliance with Romanism for the subversion
of the national Church, are not arrayed against
it on account of its doctrines, but because it is a
religious Establishment ; and they would not consent to the setting up of another form of religion,
especially such a form as Romanism, as a religious
Establishment in its place. Romanism, as has been
already shown [1], disqualifies itself by its principles
for being accepted as a religious Establishment, especially in an Empire like our own. And Romanism
itself, which hopes to be one day dominant in Ireland,
now waives all claim to State-endowment there, as
well knowing that they who are now leagued with

---

[1] Sermon iii. pp. 38, 39.

it for the subversion of the national Church, and whose
aid it desires for that purpose, would become its strenu-
ous opponents, if it aspired to be the religious Establishment of that country.

The question also is *not*—

Whether the Established Church of Ireland should
be deprived of *a portion* of its revenues, in order that
they may be applied to other purposes.

Formerly, indeed, it assumed that shape: but after
careful inquiry it was found, that if the Church of
Ireland is to be maintained as the religious Establishment of the country, its revenues are not too great for
the purpose [2], and ought to be increased rather than
diminished [3].

Therefore, the question is now simplified, and pre-
sents itself in this plain form [4]—

Ought Ireland to have a national religious Establishment? Ought the Church of Ireland to be pre-

[2] The average net income of the Clergy—of the beneficed
Clergy—is not 250*l.* a year.

[3] The evidence as to the slender provision for the Irish Clergy
may be seen in the Archbishop of Armagh's Charge for 1865,
p. 10; and in the Right Honourable Sir J. Napier's valuable
paper on the Position of the Church in Ireland, p. 13; and in the
Two Lectures on the Church in Ireland, by the Right Honourable Sir J. Whiteside, pp. 154—157, where accurate tables of the
present revenues of the Bishops and Clergy are given.

[4] See the history of what is commonly called the Appropria-
tion Clause of 1834, as related by Mr. Justice Shee, "On the
Irish Church," London, 1852, pp. 17—20, and the statement
there quoted of Mr. George Lewis Smyth,—"To suppose that
so unequal a state of things was to be composed by divert-
ing some 50,000*l.* or 100,000*l.* a year from the Irish Church
to the *purpose of education* or any thing else, was a childish
dream," and the still more important declaration of Sir George
Cornewall Lewis, "Irish Church Question," 1836, p. 351: "The
objections of the Roman Catholics to the Established Church of
Ireland would not be removed by the abolition of a few bishoprics
or the paring down of a few benefices, they lie against its very
existence." This applies still more strongly and more generally
to the advocates of the voluntary system, the members of the
Liberation Society. . Cp. Sir J. Napier on the Position of the
Irish Church, p. 10.

served as the religious Establishment of that country ?
or ought it to be deprived of its revenues, and to be
degraded from its position ?

That national Establishments of True Religion are
pleasing to Almighty God, and bring down His blessings, spiritual and temporal, upon those who maintain
them, is evident from His Holy Word. " All power
is given unto Me," says Christ, " in heaven and earth [5]."
He is " King of kings, and Lord of lords [6]." " All
Kings shall bow down before Him, all Nations shall
do Him service [7]." He is the Arbiter of the destiny of
Nations. And therefore the royal Psalmist says, " Be
wise now, therefore, O ye kings [8]; be instructed, ye
that are judges of the earth; Kiss the Son" (that is,
do homage to Christ), " lest He be angry, and so ye
perish from the right way, when His wrath is kindled
but a little." And the promise of Christ to His
Church is, " Kings shall be thy nursing fathers, and
Queens thy nursing mothers [9];" and the song of
triumph will one day sound on high through the vault
of heaven, " The kingdom of this world is become the
kingdom of our Lord and of His Christ [10]."

Assuredly, it must be most blessed for men and
Nations to do, what Christ Himself commands to be
done, and which, when done, will be celebrated with
praise and thanksgiving by the angels of God.

From such passages of Scripture it is evident that
every Country which has not a national Establishment of True Religion ought to endeavour to have
one, if it desires to enjoy God's favour ; and that every
Country which has such an Establishment, ought to
endeavour to improve it ; and that any Country which
has such an Establishment, and does not maintain, but
destroy it, falls away from God, and forfeits His blessing, without which there can be no peace in this world,
and no happiness in another.

[5] Matt. xxviii. 18.
[7] Ps. lxxii. 11.
[9] Isa. xlix. 23.

[6] Rev. xix. 16.
[8] Ps. ii. 10.
[10] Rev. xi. 15.

1. But it is said, even by some who acknowledge the truth of these principles, that the Church of Ireland ought not to be maintained as the religious Establishment of that country: the Church of Ireland, they affirm, is comparatively a *new Institution ;* it was founded, they say, on proscription and violence, and was forced upon a reluctant people three centuries ago, by the power of England, at the Reformation ; and it has therefore no just claim to be maintained as the religious Establishment of Ireland.

To this allegation we reply, that the Church of Ireland is not a new Institution ; its doctrines are the doctrines of Holy Scripture, and of the primitive Church ; its form of Church government is that of ancient Christendom ; its religion—as we have already shown—is that which was preached by St. Patrick[1], the Apostle of Ireland, more than 1300 years ago. The Reformation in Ireland was not an introduction of any thing new, but a restoration of what was old. The Bishops of the Church of Ireland at that time accepted it[2].   The Bishops of the present national Church of Ireland are the legitimate and only successors of St. Patrick and his followers in Ireland.   The present Romish Episcopate in Ireland was schismatically intruded by the Papacy into Ireland, from Spain and Italy, about 250 years ago, in opposition to the true successors of St. Patrick and of the Apostles of Christ.

These are facts which cannot be gainsaid.

2. But it is rejoined, that " the *Reformation has been rejected by* Ireland ; it has *failed in Ireland ;*" and, therefore, the Church of Ireland, which teaches the doctrines of the Reformation, ought not to be upheld as the religious Establishment of that country.

To this allegation a reply, in part, has been already

---

[1] Above, Sermon i. pp. 14—16.

[2] Above, Sermon iii., and the evidence given in Occasional Sermons on the History of the Irish Church, pp. 187. 195. 206 —218.

given [3]. The Reformation has *not* been *rejected* by Ireland; for it has *never* yet been fairly offered to Ireland. The Reformation has not failed in Ireland. The Reformation was a restoration of God's Truth. God's Truth has not failed; and cannot fail. But those persons failed who managed its concerns in Ireland. England failed, miserably failed, in her duty to God's Truth and to Ireland at that time. England had been the first to introduce Romanism into Ireland in the twelfth century [4], for the sake of her own temporal aggrandizement. And we have shown that at the Reformation, in the sixteenth century, England, who had then chief rule in Ireland, denied to Ireland the use of God's Word and of Public Prayer in the Irish language. England, Protestant England [5], imitated the practice of Papal Rome, and refused to the people of Ireland the Scriptures and a Liturgy in their own mother tongue.

In order to promote—as she fondly imagined—her own political interests, she proscribed the use of the Irish language in the worship of God. To serve her own worldly ends, she was untrue to God, to Ireland, and to herself. She made severe, but abortive, laws against Irish Roman Catholics, which made them more obstinate, but she did little to win them by milder measures to a purer faith.

England also failed in her duty to God and His Church in Ireland in another respect. At the Reformation, Tithes were taken from the dissolved Monasteries, but they were not restored, as they ought to have been, to the parishes from which they accrued. They were given to English noblemen and other laymen, and to the English Crown. Two English Sovereigns, King James I. and King Charles I., set a bright example to lay impropriators, by restoring impropriations to the Church, and succouring the poor Clergy; but the evil still remains; through the unhappy policy of Eng-

---

[3] Above, Sermon iii. pp. 48—50.   [4] Above, Sermon ii. p. 32.
[5] Above, Sermon iii. p. 49.

land, the Church of Ireland still groans under the
burden of lay impropriations [6].

Besides, England failed in her duty to God, to the
Gospel, and to Ireland in another important respect
also, especially in the eighteenth century. She used
the Church of God in Ireland as a secular engine of
her own State-policy. She discouraged the native
Irish Clergy, and she checked the supply of faithful
and zealous Pastors in Ireland, by bestowing Irish
Bishoprics on English Ecclesiastics, who knew nothing of the Irish language, and cared little for the
Irish people; and who were not qualified by piety and
learning for their sacred office, and whose chief recom-
mendation was, that they were eager political partisans
of what by a strange misnomer was called " the English
interest in Ireland"—as if the interest of England could
be promoted by treachery to God! Some of these
English Prelates never resided in their Irish dioceses ;
and they gave the best benefices to their English re-
latives, who were also non-resident [7].

England also failed in her duty to God's Church in
Ireland in another matter. She took little care to
provide a resident Clergy for that country. In the
year 1710, there was no residence for one Pastor in
ten in Ireland. And this state of things continued
for the greater part of the eighteenth century [8].

Brethren, with such evidence as this before us, are
we not bound to say, that it is not the Reformation
that has been rejected in Ireland? no, but its principles
have been rejected by England, and it has never been
fairly offered to Ireland. It is not the Reformation that
has failed in Ireland, but we have failed, lamentably
failed, in our duty to Ireland and to God. And when

[6] See Occasional Sermons, pp. 251—256.
[7] Abundant evidence of this may be seen in Maguire's Letters
on the Church of Ireland, 1850: Letter xi. Bp. Mant's History of the Church of Ireland, ii. 252. Primate Boulter's Letters,
1770.
[8] Abp. of Dublin's Charge, 1865, p. 26. Cp. Occasional Sermons,
p. 251.

we consider how much we have failed in our duty to
God, to the Reformation, and to Ireland, the wonder is,
not that the Church of Ireland should not be more
prosperous than it is, and that the Reformation should
not have made more progress. Rather we may be sur-
prised that, notwithstanding the failings of England,
and the hostility of Rome, and the sacrilegious covetousness of some of Ireland's own children, encouraged
by the example of England, and robbing [9] God and
His Church, and forcing many of her members to
emigrate to foreign [1] lands, and thus thinning her
ranks, and impoverishing the Christian Ministry, and
necessitating the union of many parishes in one benefice; and notwithstanding the culpable neglect and
disorderly licence and irregular extravagance of others,
even among the Clergy themselves, breaking the unity
of the Church, and making her a scorn and byword to
her enemies, the Church of Ireland should exist in her
present efficiency, and be advancing steadily on as
she is [2].

And yet,—strange to say,—there are some persons
in England who impute to God's Truth the consequences of England's sins. Many there are in England,
who taunt the Church of Ireland with the fewness of
her members, which is due to England's unfaithfulness;
and they would even punish her by spoliation on ac-

---

[9] E. g. by the abolition of the Tithe of agistment by the
Irish Parliament in 1735. On this and other hindrances to the
Church, see Occasional Sermons, p. 252. To this may be added
the excision of a quarter of the revenue of the Church by the
Tithe Commutation Act of 1838.

[1] See Phelan's Remains, ii. 45, 46.

[2] "Our churches have well-nigh trebled in number within the
last century, and are yearly multiplying: the ministers of our
Church have increased in like proportion," Archbishop of Armagh's Charge, 1865, p. 22; and this, though the population of
Ireland has greatly decreased in the last quarter of a century. In
the year 1730, the Clergy of the Church of Ireland were 800; in
the year 1863, they had increased to 2281. In the year 1730,
the Churches were only 400; in the year 1863, they had increased to 1633.

count of that fewness, which we ourselves have caused!
Brethren, King Herod of Jewry might as well have in-
sulted the mothers of Bethlehem for their childlessness,
after he himself had massacred their infants. He might
as well have pillaged their houses, and dismantled the
walls of Bethlehem, and sold their stones by auction, on
the plea that because of its depopulation by the murder
of the Innocents, they were no longer necessary to be
kept up!

Rather let us confess and amend our faults. We
owe a debt to God and His Truth. We have hindered
its progress in Ireland, we ought to accelerate it. We
received the blessings of the Gospel from Ireland in
ancient times[3]. And we have inflicted many wrongs
upon her. Let us not aggravate our sin by despoiling
her. We owe a debt of reparation to Ireland. We
were the first to Romanize her, we ought now to do all
in our power to evangelize her.

3. But it is objected by some, that the past cannot be
undone, and that we must deal with facts as they are.
Look (they say) at the last census of Ireland. Ireland
contains about five millions and three-quarters[4] of

---

[3] Sermon ii. pp. 22, 23.

[4] Correct reports of the results of the census of Ireland are
quoted in the Rev. Dr. A. T. Lee's seasonable publication, "Facts
respecting the Present State of the Church in Ireland," 1865, p. 7.

	1834.	1861.	De-crease.	In-crease.	Per Cent.
Established Church .... including Methodists.....................	853,160 —	693,357 } 45,399 }	114,404		13·4
Roman Catholics..............	6,436,060	4,505,265	1,930,795		30·4
Presbyterian .... and other Protestant Dissenters.........	643,058 21,882	523,291 76,661	119,767 ...	54,839	18·6 251·3
	7,954,160	5,798,967	2,164,966	54,839	...
Corrected return of Pro- } testant Dissenters .... }	21,882	16,990	4,892	...	22·4

inhabitants. Of these, four and a half millions are Roman Catholics. The Established Church of Ireland does not number a million of souls. Is it not (it is asked) a monstrous injustice, that a Church so barren of fruit should be allowed to cumber the ground, that it should even be maintained as the Established Church of that country; and that they who do not derive any benefit from it, and who reject its ministrations, should be forced to assist in maintaining it?

What, brethren, is to be said here?

We do not disparage the evidence derived from Tables of Population. Blessed is the Church of God which preaches His Truth to willing ears, and can say, pointing to a large and loving offspring, " Behold I and the children whom the Lord hath given me [5]."

But we deny that Tables of Population afford any adequate test and right criterion, whether a Church ought to be established, or whether, when established, it ought or ought not to be maintained.

Time was, of old, when the visible Church of God on earth dwindled down to one small family. It floated on a wilderness of waters in the Ark, which contained only eight souls. But no one will say that the religion of that small household was not true, or was not to be accepted as the religion of the world. Time was, of old, when the visible Church of God was reduced to a despised remnant, and was represented by the burning Bush in the silent solitudes of Horeb— burning, but not consumed; for the Angel of the Lord was in it. Time was, of old, many centuries after the delivery of the Law from Sinai, that the visible Church of God seemed to have scarcely any living form and utterance except in the prophet Elijah; but no one will say that the religion which Elijah taught was not to be the national religion of Israel. The fire which came down from heaven on Carmel proclaimed it, and the people themselves owned it,—" The Lord,

[5] Isa. viii. 18.

He is the God; the Lord, He is the God[e]." In the
days of Christ upon earth, the Gospel was like a grain
of mustard seed; but it was to overshadow the Earth.
It was like a little leaven, but it was to leaven the World.
The Church was a little flock, but all nations of the
World are to become one fold under one Shepherd.
On the other hand, brethren, we see in Holy Scripture
a dark picture, which ought to be a warning to ourselves. In the Book of Revelation we behold the por-
traiture of a false and corrupt Church, beguiling men
by her allurements, and destroying their souls by her
idolatries, and whose destiny it is to be burnt with fire.
And of this false and corrupt Church it is expressly
said, that it contains large numbers in its Communion.
Multitudes are enrolled in its Census. Myriads upon
myriads swell its Tables of Population. "The waters
which thou sawest, upon which the harlot sitteth,"
enthroned as a Queen (we read), "are," that is, they
represent, "peoples, and multitudes, and nations, and
tongues[f]." Of this, therefore, we may be sure, that
Tables of Population are very fallacious, when applied
to the question before us.

Besides, brethren, what are Tables of Population?
What is a Census? It is an enumeration of human
beings. And what are human generations? Their
breath is in God's hand. They are like leaves on the
trees in autumn, quivering on the bough for a while,
eddying in the air, and then falling to the earth and
strewing the ground. God can wither them in a mo-
ment. He often sweeps them away by Plague, Pesti-
lence, and Famine; or they disappear by emigration.
By one breath of His mouth He disturbs all our calcu-
lations which are grounded on Tables of Population.

Look at Ireland herself. In 1851, her population
was not so large as it had been thirty years before[g].

[e] 1 Kings xviii. 39. [f] Rev. xvii. 15.

Population of Ireland:			
In 1821	6,801,827	In 1841	8,175,124
1831	7,767,401	1851	6,515,794
		1861	5,798,987

Twenty-five years ago, Ireland contained more than eight millions of souls. But in 1861, she numbered only five millions and three-quarters. She lost more than two millions of her people in twenty years. In 1834, there were about six and a half millions of Roman Catholics in Ireland; but in 1861 they had dwindled down to four and a half millions. And it is doubtful whether there are as many. It is notorious (as Romish Priests themselves complain) [9], that as soon as they cross the Atlantic many of them cease to profess that religion. Romanism has lost two millions in Ireland in about twenty-five years. And it is certain, that though all classes of religionists have decreased greatly in Ireland during the last quarter of a century,—and if matters go on as they have done, Ireland herself may soon be almost depopulated,—yet the members of the Established Church have decreased *far less* in proportion than those of any other religious profession.

These Tables of Population ebb and flow like the rolling billows of the restless sea. Will any wise man build his reasonings concerning religion on the fickle fluctuations of such an Euripus as that? Are its wavering undulations to be set against that which has no ebb and flow, but remains for ever crystallized in a pure, deep, eternal calm,—the Word of God? Is the ship of the State to be drifted about by veering gusts and shifting currents, and not to be steered with a firm hand, by the unerring chart and compass of God's Word within her, and by the light of the fixed stars above her? If this be the case, alas for her and for her crew! She must split and founder upon rocks, or else be stranded on quicksands. There is no surer sign of moral decline in statesmanship, and of religious de-

[9] As the Dublin Review says, July, 1865, p. 228,—" We fear that there can be little doubt that in the United States the [Roman Catholic] Church loses more souls than it gains. In the second generation the faith of the [Roman] Catholic immigrant is constantly lost."

F

generacy and degradation in nations, than when men's minds are enslaved by the gross materialism of Numbers, Time, and Space, instead of holding spiritual commerce and communion with the unseen world. There is no surer sign of decay in Governments and States, than when men, who ought to lead others, begin to gauge moral Truths by mechanical standards, and set themselves to measure holy things—such as the existence of national Churches — by the capricious ciphers of Time, and not by the unchanging truths of Eternity. And there is no surer sign of a great and noble mind, than to cling loyally to Truth, when it is scorned, forsaken, and persecuted by the world.

4. But we are not yet allowed to have done with Tables of Population.

It is objected by the opponents of the Church of Ireland, that there are many Parishes in that country, where the members of the Established Church are *very few*, and that therefore she ought not to be maintained as the national Church.

This objection involves many fallacies.

(1) There is scarcely a single benefice in Ireland where there are no members of the Established Church[1].

(2) Though there are some benefices in which the members of the Church are few, it by no means follows that the Church should be despoiled of her revenues, to the detriment of her people who dwell in benefices where her members are not few.

(3) Is it any where revealed in Scripture that God does not care for a few? Christ left the ninety and nine, to seek and to save the one[2]. "There is joy in heaven over one sinner that repenteth[3]." A single soul is worth more than worlds of matter. If the Church of Ireland is not a true Church of Christ, then, in heaven's name, let her perish! But, if she is, then Christ is with her; and no congregation can be called small where Christ is. No persons are to be despised

---

[1] See Dr. Lee's "Facts," &c., pp. 9, 10.
[2] Matt. xviii. 12.   [3] Luke xv. 7.

as few, who enjoy the presence of Him who is Infinite and Eternal. Hear His own words : " Where *two or three* are gathered together in My Name, there am I in the midst of them⁴." We do not hesitate to say, that the two or three faithful worshippers—be they aged men or women, or poor children—joining together in prayer to God, and offering to Him a reasonable service, and listening to the pure Word of God preached to them in the parish churches of Ireland, are far more pleasing to God than large and crowded congregations which offer prayer and praise to other objects of adoration besides Him ; and they may avert from a nation His wrath, which is provoked by creature-worship, and may bring down His blessing upon it.

If the Church of Ireland preaches the Gospel of Christ, if she dispenses His Sacraments by an Apostolic Ministry, do not, I entreat you, anger God by despising and despoiling those few worshippers, because they are few. Remember Christ's fearful malediction : " It were better that a millstone were hanged about a man's neck, and he cast into the depths of the sea, than that he should offend *one* of these little ones⁵." Rather cherish them the more, because they are few. Their fewness is due, in a great measure, to our sins. " Destroy not the cluster on the vine, for a blessing is in it⁶." And you will be blessed by Him who said, " Inasmuch as ye have done it to *one* of the least of these my brethren, ye have done it to Me⁷."

5. But we may go further. If the Church of Ireland is a true Church of Christ, as we have shown her to be ; if she holds and teaches the true faith ; if she is the rightful representative of the ancient Church of Ireland, then we do not hesitate to say, that there is not a single person in Ireland, whether Protestant or Roman Catholic, who does not in a certain sense belong to her.

Let us not be betrayed into the fallacy of deciding

⁴ Matt. xviii. 20.   ⁵ Matt. xviii. 6.
. ⁶ Isa. lxv. 8.   ⁷ Matt. xxv. 40.

questions of Church-membership by Tables of Population, and not by the Word of God and by sound principles of theology. "Judge not according to the
appearance, but judge righteous judgment."

Consider, brethren; What is a true Church? She
is no other than the "Body of Christ[8]." All His
members are hers. Some may be sounder members
than others. But, so far as they hold the true Faith,
and receive the Word of God and His Sacraments, so
far they belong to her; so far as they are Christians,
they belong to Christ; and so far as they belong to
Christ, they belong to Christ's Church. Is the Church of
Ireland a true Church? Is she the true Church of that
country, or is she not? Doubtless she is. Are Roman
Catholics Christians, or are they not? If they are, then
we do not scruple to affirm, that, as far as they are so,
they belong to the true Church of Ireland. There is no
other way of becoming a Christian except by the Word
and Sacraments of Christ. And the Word and Sacraments of Christ are the dowry of His Church. By
whomsoever they are administered, they are hers, because she is Christ's Body and Spouse. It is notorious
that many of the Roman Catholic peasantry of Ireland
look to the Protestant Pastor of the Parish as their
best friend. But even if it were true that the Roman
Catholics of Ireland ignore the Church of Ireland,
and even though they may reject her ministrations, and
desire her destruction, yet still the truth remains, they
are her children; she owes motherly love and motherly
care to them, and they owe a filial duty to her[9].

6. But again; it is alleged to be very unjust, that
the Church of Ireland should be maintained by payments of Roman Catholics who *derive no benefit* from
her.

What shall we say here? Our reply is,—

[8] Eph. i. 23. Col. i. 24.
[9] These principles have been further confirmed and illustrated
from Holy Scripture and the ancient Fathers of the Church, in
"Theophilus Anglicanus," part iii. chap. iii.

(1) That a large portion of the endowments were given to her by Protestants [1], and,—

(2) That almost all the property in Ireland—eight-ninths of the whole—from which tithe is paid, is in the hands of Protestants, and not of Roman Catholics.

But (3) we do not rest on such arguments as these;

We do not hesitate to affirm that *no tithe at all* is paid from *Roman Catholics* to the *Church of Ireland*. Our assertion is this : Tithe may be paid in some cases *through* them, but in no single instance is it paid *from* them. They may in some cases be the *channels through* which the payment is made; but they are not the *sources from* which that which is paid springs. The Tithe-*payer* is not the Tithe-*owner*. All this is perfectly clear from the single consideration, that if all the Tithes of the Church of Ireland were taken away from her to-morrow, not a shilling of them would be given to the Tithe-payer. A few years since, it was proposed to despoil the Church of Ireland of part of her revenues, but no one ever dreamt that the supposed surplus, of which she was to be robbed, would be given to Roman Catholic or any other Tithe-payers, but it was to be applied to general instruction in Ireland. And at this present time also, when some Roman Catholic leaders have thought fit to combine with a very different class of religionists in an endeavour to deprive the Irish Church of her tithes, it is not proposed by any one that any of those Tithes should be given to Roman Catholic Tithe-payers; which surely ought to be the case, *if* Tithes are really *owned* by those through whom they are *paid* [2].

The fact is,—the overthrow of the Church of Ireland, as a national Establishment, is desired by Romanists, because she is the strongest bulwark against

---

[1] See Dr. Lee's Facts, pp. 5, 6.

[2] On this point compare the Rt. Hon. Sir J. Napier's observations in his paper on the Position of the Irish Church, 1865, pp. 9, 10.

Romish dogmas and Romish domination; and her subversion is aimed at by others of a very different character, as a preparation to the destruction of all Church
Establishments. And if these two parties should gain
their purpose, then, when they have done so, they will
tear one another and the country in pieces by deadly
feuds.

7. And here we come to another count of the indict-
ment against the Church of Ireland.

She ought not, it is said, to be maintained as the
national Church of that country, because so many
persons there are alienated from her, and *derive no
benefit* from her.

If this argument were sound, then no religious
national Establishment could ever be maintained. The
argument which is good against the Church in Ireland
to-day, will be equally good against the Church in
Wales to-morrow, and against the Church of England
the day after.

There is not a Christian Establishment in any
nation in which a large portion of the people are not
indifferent or even hostile to it. Christ Himself and
His Apostles have foretold this [3]. The latter days—
the days before His second coming—will be days of
worldliness, unbelief, and apostasy.

But if the Church of Ireland is, as we affirm, a true
Church of Christ, then we do not scruple to say that
she is a blessing, not only to those who love her, but
to those who would destroy her. She is a blessing to
the country at large.

What does Holy Scripture teach here? The men of
Sodom hated Lot, and reviled him, saying, " This fel-
low came in to sojourn, and he will needs be a judge [4]."
But, if there had been nine other men in Sodom like
Lot, then Sodom would not have been destroyed [5].
The house of Potiphar prospered, because Joseph was

---

[3] Matt. xxiv. 4—12. 21—24. 37. 2 Thess. ii. 3. 2 Tim. iii. 1.
2 Pet. iii. 3. 1 John ii. 18. Jude 18.
[4] Gen. xix. 9.   [5] Gen. xviii. 32.

there [6]. The presence of the Ark brought a blessing from heaven on the house of Obed-edom [7]. God gave to St. Paul the lives of all them who were with him in the ship [8]. So we doubt not that the presence of the Church in Ireland, preaching the pure Gospel of Christ, and ministering His holy Sacraments, is—whether men own it or no—a source of inestimable blessing to Ireland ; and the destruction of that Church as a national Establishment would be a curse to those who destroy it.

Consider also this. It is true that the Bishops, and Clergy, and laity of the Church of Ireland are a small minority as compared with those Bishops, and Clergy, and laity in that land who own the supremacy of Rome. But what is the first duty of a Church ? To diffuse the Light of God's Word. And therefore a Church is symbolized in Holy Scripture by a seven-branched golden candlestick [9]. And what is the use of the candlestick of a Church, if the wicks of its lamps are clotted and fungous, and if its pipes are clogged up with the sediment and dregs of corrupt traditions, and if the liquid oil of Scriptural truth does not flow freshly and freely through them, and it does not dispense spiritual light, and the atmosphere around is gloomy, murky, and fetid ? Its doom is, to be removed by Christ, who walks among the golden candlesticks and observes them [1]. And what has the Church of Rome in Ireland done for diffusing the light of God's Word there ? With her superior number of Bishops and Priests, and with the vast crowd of hungry multitudes needing to be taught, she might reasonably be expected to have done much. But is it so ? Has she promoted the spread of God's Truth? Has she not hindered it ? Has she encouraged the circulation of the Scriptures ? Has she not obstructed it ? Can the Church of Rome in Ireland, with her boasted majority of Bishops, Priests, and people, point to a single

[6] Gen. xxxix. 3.
[8] Acts xxvii. 24.
[1] Rev. i. 13.
[7] 2 Sam. vi. 11.
[9] See Rev. i. 12, 13. 20.

theological work of acknowledged celebrity which she has ever produced in Ireland for the elucidation of Holy Scripture? I know not of any[2]. What then would be the condition of Ireland, if she were to be left, for a supply of spiritual light, to the candlestick of the Church of Rome? She would be plunged in spiritual darkness.

On the other hand, the national Church of Ireland, despised though she be by many, as a puny and paltry minority (and the fewer her numbers are, " the greater share of glory"), has never been wanting, and God grant she never may be, in bright spiritual luminaries. She has had her Usshers, her Bedells, her Bramhalls, her Jeremy Taylors, her Boyles, her Berkeleys, her Edmund Burke, and her Alexander Knox. She has had her Hales, her Graves, her Magees, her Jebbs, her Elringtons, her Phelans, her Archer Butlers, her M'Cauls, her Brinkleys, and her Robinsons; and she has many others, whose names will occur to you—especially one most dear to the Church of West-minster, and a distinguished ornament of this Univer-sity; and in them it has been clearly proved that there is no restraint to the Lord to save by many or by few[3]. And of late years she has been very zealous in her endeavours to diffuse the spiritual light of the Holy Scriptures throughout the land.

Brethren, Egypt was much larger and far more populous than Goshen. But who, that had eyes to see, would prefer the darkness of Egypt to the light of Goshen? In comparing the Church of Ireland and her claims with those of the Church of Rome in that country, do not be deluded by Tables of Population. Do not contrast their numbers; but place the two Candlesticks side by side, and ask yourselves this question,—Which of the two Candlesticks diffuses

---

[2] One work has been mentioned to me by a friend in answer to this question;—an Exposition of St. Paul's Epistles, by the Rev. J. McEvilly, President of St. Jarlath's, Tuam, 1856. But this is, I fear, a solitary exception; and serves to make the fact above stated more remarkable.   [3] 1 Sam. xiv. 6.

more light around it? And be assured that the Church which shines most brightly, is most pleasing to the God of Light and Truth, and ought to be maintained by man.

8. Once more. The Tithes and Endowments of the Church of Ireland do not belong to the State of England, nor do they belong to the Roman Catholics of Ireland, nor do they belong to the Protestants of Ireland, nor do they belong to the Church of Ireland, except as their usufructuary and trustee. But they belong to ALMIGHTY GOD. They have been solemnly dedicated to Him. This act of dedication has been confirmed in the most sacred manner by the English nation. That confirmation is engrafted on the Coronation Oath, taken by her Sovereigns, speaking in God's presence, in His house, before His altar, and holding His Scriptures in their hands. It utters its voice in the legislative Act of Union with Ireland. It speaks in oaths of abjuration. If there is such a thing as a solemn pledge upon earth, if there is such a thing as a holy vow registered in heaven, it is that which the British nation has taken, to maintain inviolate that property which has been consecrated to Almighty God, for the use of His Church in Ireland.

Brethren, are we prepared to rob God? Are we prepared to commit sacrilege? Are we prepared to imitate the sin, and to incur the penalty of Achan in the Old Testament, and of Ananias and Sapphira in the New? Are we prepared to imitate Herod Agrippa, who "stretched forth his hands to vex certain of the Church[4]," and was smitten by an Angel, and was eaten up of worms and died[5]? Are we prepared to make war against God? Are we prepared to take up arms against Him, whose armies are Plagues and Pestilences, Famines and Wars, civil and foreign? If so, hearken to His words, "Ye have robbed Me. But ye say, Wherein have we robbed Thee? In Tithes and offerings. Ye are cursed with a curse. Ye have

[4] Acts xii. 1.   [5] Acts xii. 23.

robbed Me; even this whole nation⁶." God sent
a three years' famine on Israel⁷. And why? because
Saul their king had killed the Gibeonites. And who
were the Gibeonites? The meanest of God's ministers;
the hewers of wood and drawers of water in His Ta-
bernacle. And will He not much more punish those
who dare to rob Him in His Church? Will not they
be made to feel the wrath of Christ, who is "KING of
kings and LORD of lords⁸," and who said to him who
persecuted His Church, "Saul, Saul, why persecutest
thou ME⁹?"

9. Brethren, the times in which we live are times
of severe trial. And it may haply be, that times
of severer trial await you, my younger friends, who
are soon about to enter on the duties of active
life. The present times are times of trial, because
they prove what men really are. They sift men
through and through. They show whether they have
faith in God. They prove whether men believe that
God is the Governor of the world and the Judge of
human actions, and that His Truth will finally prevail.

Let us not be perplexed by what we see around us.
Let us not be staggered by the power and prosperity
of evil. Christ Himself " came to His own, and His own
received Him not." He was rejected by the World and
crucified. But He raised Himself from the dead, and
ascended in triumph into heaven; and He will come
again with great glory to judge the quick and dead,
and to reward His faithful servants, and to put all
enemies under His feet. The course of Christ in this
world was a foreshadowing of the course of His Word
and of His Church upon Earth. The Word of God,
the Church of God, they also will have their Gethse-
mane and their Calvary. But they too, like Christ,
will have their day of Resurrection, and their day of
glorious Ascension. They " who suffer with Him on
earth, will reign with Him" for ever in heaven.

⁶ Mal. iii. 7. 9.   ⁷ 2 Sam. xxi. 1.
⁸ Rev. xvii. 14; xix. 16.   ⁹ Acts ix. 4.

Therefore, dearly beloved, "judge not according to the appearance, but judge righteous judgment." Prefer not popular fallacies to unpopular truths. Do not be too eager to be on the winning side in this world. Look forward, and look upward. Remember the end. In this question concerning the Church of God in Ireland, and in all similar questions which are now trying the faith and moral courage of many among us both in Church and State, ask not yourselves what men think, or what men say; but ask yourselves what is in accordance with the Will of God, and with the Word of God. Men will not be our judges at the bar of Christ; but all men will be judged by Him. And "the Word which He hath spoken, that will judge us at the Last Day [1]. Even in this present world, as we have seen in tracing the history of Christianity in Ireland, the violation of great principles is followed by severe retribution. And it needs no gift of prophecy to foretell, that if the measures should be adopted which are now devised against the Church of Ireland, many of those who eagerly abet them will be the first to rue their results. The Church of Ireland is the true Church of Christ in that country. She is the faithful teacher of religion and of loyalty. She is the best safeguard of order and law. A Christian Church with an open Bible and a Scriptural Liturgy, is the best defence of a nation. And if she is overthrown, then it is greatly to be feared that we may see a war in Ireland of religion against religion, of race against race, of Democracy against Monarchy, of socialism against property, of turbulence against law, of anarchy against order, and, it may be, eventually of fanaticism and infidelity against Christianity itself. And then England may see Ireland converted into a hostile fortress against us, from which a foreign foe may spring forth upon us, and assail us in our homes.

Almighty God Himself now speaks to us and says, Sow not the wind, lest ye reap the whirlwind. Dis-

[1] John xii. 48.

mantle not your own fortress. Pluck not down your own house. Snap not the golden chain asunder which binds Ireland to England. Discourage not your best friends, alienate not your most faithful allies. Bestow not prizes on faction, and give not a triumph to sedition. But cherish, improve, and strengthen the true Scriptural, primitive, Catholic, and Apostolic Church of Ireland. Have faith in God. He now tries you by difficulties. Your difficulties are His opportunities; your midnight is His noon. Have faith in Him. Obey Him. Then He who said, One man of you shall chase a thousand[2], and who would not use the 32,000 men of Gideon in order to vanquish the countless myriads of Midianites, but who winnowed them down to 300, and by those 300 gained the victory, will add fresh glory to England by means of the Church of Ireland, and will unite the two countries for ever, by the hands of Christ Himself, in the indissoluble bonds of Truth, and Love, and Peace.

10. Lastly, whatever may be the issue in this short and fleeting world, yet of this we may be sure, that no labour in the cause of God can be in vain. It is above chance, and beyond failure. When all earthly empires shall have passed away as a dream, when the earth itself shall be dissolved, and the elements shall melt with fervent heat[3], when the visible Church on earth shall have finished her course, and Christ Himself shall appear on the clouds of heaven with power and great glory, and call all men from their graves; then all who have been true to Him in times of trial and defection will have their portion for ever in the Church triumphant and glorified, and will be enrolled as citizens in the everlasting census of the heavenly Jerusalem, and will receive from His hands a palm of victory, and a crown of glory, which fadeth not away.

[2] Josh. xxiii. 10.   [3] 2 Pet. iii. 10.

GILBERT AND RIVINGTON, PRINTERS, ST. JOHN'S SQUARE, LONDON.

PUBLICATIONS BY CHR. WORDSWORTH, D.D.

ARCHDEACON OF WESTMINSTER.

THE GREEK TESTAMENT, with Introductions and Notes.

Part I. THE FOUR GOSPELS. *Sixth Edition.* 1*l.* 1*s.*

II. THE ACTS OF THE APOSTLES. *Fifth Edition.* 10*s.* 6*d.*

III. ST. PAUL's EPISTLES. *Fifth Edition.* 1*l.* 11*s.* 6*d.*

IV. THE GENERAL EPISTLES, AND THE BOOK OF REVELA-TION, and Indexes to the whole work. *Third Edition.* 1*l.* 1*s.* Each Part is complete in itself. Any of the Parts may be had separately.

THE OLD TESTAMENT in the Authorized Version; with Notes and Introductions.

Part I. GENESIS and EXODUS. *Second Edition.* 1*l.* 1*s.*

II. LEVITICUS, NUMBERS, DEUTERONOMY. *Second Edition.* 18*s.*

III. JOSHUA, JUDGES, RUTH. *Second Edition.* 12*s.*

IV. THE BOOKS OF SAMUEL. *Second Edition.* 10*s.*

V. THE BOOKS OF KINGS, CHRONICLES, EZRA, NEHEMIAH, ESTHER. *Second Edition.* 1*l.* 1*s.*

VI. THE BOOK OF JOB. *Second Edition.* 9*s.*

VII. THE BOOK OF PSALMS. *Second Edition.* 15*s.*

VIII. PROVERBS, ECCLESIASTES, SONG OF SOLOMON. 12*s.*

Other Parts are in preparation. Any Part may be had separately.

ON THE INSPIRATION OF THE BIBLE. *Fifth Edition.* 1*s.*

ON THE INTERPRETATION OF THE BIBLE. 3*s.* 6*d.*

THE' HOLY YEAR; or, Original Hymns for Sundays, Holy Days, and Daily Use, throughout the Year: with a Preface on Hymnology. *Fourth Edition.* *Price* 6*d.*, with a discount of 25 per cent. to the Clergy, Schools, &c.

The HOLY YEAR; Musical Edition, with APPROPRIATE TUNES, edited by W. H. MONK. 4*s.* 6*d.*

Editions of the HOLY YEAR in larger type. 4*s.* 6*d.* 2*s.* 6*d.*

THEOPHILUS ANGLICANUS; or, Manual of Instruction in the Principles of the Church Universal and of the Church of England. *Ninth Edition.* 5*s.*

ELEMENTS OF INSTRUCTION ON THE CHURCH; being an Abridgment of the above. 2s.

MANUAL OF CONFIRMATION. *Fourth Edit.* 9d.

S. HIPPOLYTUS AND THE CHURCH OF ROME in the beginning of the Third Century, from the newly-discovered "Philosophumena." 8s. 6d.

LETTERS TO M. GONDON, on the DESTRUCTIVE CHARACTER of the CHURCH of ROME, in RELIGION and POLITY. *Third Edition.* 7s. 6d.

A SEQUEL TO THE ABOVE. *Second Edition.* 6s. 6d.

UNION WITH ROME; or, the Question considered, "Is not the CHURCH of ROME the BABYLON of the APOCALYPSE?" *New Edition.* 1s.

THEOCRITUS, Codicum MSS. ope recensitus et emendatus, cum Indicibus locupletissimis. 10s. 6d.

ATHENS AND ATTICA. Journal of a Residence there. *Third Edition.* Crown 8vo. 8s. 6d.

GREECE, Historical, Pictorial, and Descriptive. *Fifth Edition.* 1l. 8s.

INEDITED ANCIENT WRITINGS, or GRAFFITI, Copied from the Walls of POMPEII, with Fac-similes. 2s. 6d.

CORRESPONDENCE OF RICHARD BENTLEY, D.D., Master of Trinity College, Cambridge. 2 vols. 2l. 2s.

MEMOIRS OF WILLIAM WORDSWORTH. 2 vols. 30s.

A DIARY IN FRANCE; mainly on Topics concerning Education and the Church. *Second Edition.* 5s. 6d.

NOTES AT PARIS. 1854. 4s.

KING EDWARD THE SIXTH'S LATIN GRAMMAR. *Fifteenth Edition.* 3s. 6d.

KING EDWARD THE SIXTH'S FIRST LATIN BOOK. The LATIN ACCIDENCE; including a Short Syntax and Prosody, with an ENGLISH TRANSLATION, for Junior Classes. *Third Edition.* 12mo. 2s.

OCCASIONAL SERMONS

PREACHED IN WESTMINSTER ABBEY,
BY CHR. WORDSWORTH, D.D.,
ARCHDEACON OF WESTMINSTER.

Contents of the several Numbers :—

FIRST SERIES.

1. COUNSELS AND CONSOLATIONS IN TIMES OF HERESY AND SCHISM.
2. ON PLEAS ALLEGED FOR SEPARATION FROM THE CHURCH.
3. THE DOCTRINE OF BAPTISM WITH REFERENCE TO THE OPINION OF PREVENIENT GRACE.
4. AN ENQUIRY—Whether the Baptismal Offices of the Church of England may be interpreted in a Calvinistic Sense? Part I. The Doctrine of Scripture compared with the Tenets of Calvin.
5. THE ENQUIRY CONTINUED—Whether the Baptismal Offices of the Church of England were framed by Persons holding Calvinistic Opinions; and whether they may be interpreted in a Hypothetical Sense? Part II. Argument from Internal Evidence.
6. THE ENQUIRY CONTINUED. Part III. Argument from External Evidence.
7. THE CHURCH OF ENGLAND IN 1711 AND 1850.
8. THE CHURCH OF ENGLAND AND THE CHURCH OF ROME IN 1850. Conclusion.

SECOND SERIES.

9. DIOTREPHES AND ST. JOHN; On the Claim set up by the Bishop of Rome to exercise Jurisdiction in England and Wales, by erecting therein Episcopal Sees.
10. ST. PETER AT ANTIOCH, AND THE ROMAN PONTIFF IN ENGLAND.
11. THE CHRISTIAN SOLDIER, A CHRISTIAN BUILDER.
12. ON A RECENT PROPOSAL OF THE CHURCH OF ROME TO MAKE A NEW ARTICLE OF FAITH. (The Immaculate Conception. See also No. 43.)
13. ON THE AUTHORITY AND USES OF CHURCH SYNODS.
14 & 15. ON SECESSIONS TO THE CHURCH OF ROME. 2s.
16. ON THE PRIVILEGES AND DUTIES OF THE CHRISTIAN LAITY. Conclusion.

OCCASIONAL SERMONS (*continued*).

THIRD SERIES.

17 & 18. ON THE GREAT EXHIBITION OF 1851.
19. ON SECULAR EDUCATION.
20. ON THE OFFICE OF THE HOLY SPIRIT IN EDUCATION.
21. ON THE USE OF THE CHURCH CATECHISM IN NATIONAL EDUCATION.
22. ON AN EDUCATION RATE.
23. ON INTELLECTUAL DISPLAY IN EDUCATION.
24. EARLY INSTRUCTION.

FOURTH SERIES.

25—33. ON THE HISTORY OF THE CHURCH OF IRELAND.

FIFTH SERIES.

34. RELIGIOUS RESTORATION IN ENGLAND — Introductory: On National Sins, Judgments, and Duties.
35. CENSUS OF RELIGIOUS WORSHIP.
36. THE EPISCOPATE. On Additional Sees.
37. THE DIACONATE.
38. TITHES, ENDOWMENTS, AND MAINTENANCE OF THE CLERGY.
39. ON CHURCH RATES.
40. ON DIVORCE.
41. RESTORATION OF HOLY MATRIMONY.
42. HOPES OF RELIGIOUS RESTORATION. Conclusion.

SIXTH SERIES.

43. ON THE IMMACULATE CONCEPTION. See No. 12.
44. THE CHRISTIAN SUNDAY.
45. THE ARMIES ON WHITE HORSES; OR, THE SOLDIER'S RETURN.
46—49. ON THE ACTS OF THE APOSTLES AS APPLICABLE TO THE PRESENT TIMES.
50. ON MARRIAGE WITH A PERSON DIVORCED.

SEVENTH SERIES.

51. A PLEA FOR INDIA.
52. ON THE ADDITIONAL SERVICE IN WESTMINSTER ABBEY.
53. ON "THE STATE SERVICES."
54. ON THE INSPIRATION OF THE OLD TESTAMENT.
55. ON MARRIAGE WITH A DECEASED WIFE'S SISTER.
56. ON THE ATONEMENT.
57. ELIJAH AN EXAMPLE FOR ENGLAND.

*_** *Most of the Numbers of the above may be had separately.*

RIVINGTONS;
LONDON, OXFORD, AND CAMBRIDGE.

www.ingramcontent.com/pod-product-compliance
Lightning Source LLC
Chambersburg PA
CBHW021421090426

42742CB00009B/1202